By Advice of Counsel

By Advice of Counsel

by Arthur Cheney Train

CONTENTS

THE SHYSTER
THE KID AND THE CAMEL
CONTEMPT OF COURT
BY ADVICE OF COUNSEL
"THAT SORT OF WOMAN"
YOU'RE ANOTHER!
BEYOND A REASONABLE DOUBT

The Shyster

Shyster, n. [Origin obscure.] One who does business trickily; a person without professional honor: used chiefly of lawyers; as, pettifoggers and shysters.—CENTURY DICTIONARY.

When Terry McGurk hove the brick through the window of Froelich's butcher shop he did it casually, on general principles, and without any idea of starting anything. He had strolled unexpectedly round the corner from his dad's saloon, had seen the row going on between Froelich and the gang of boys that after school hours used the street in front of the shop as a ball ground, and had merely seized the opportunity to vindicate his reputation as a desperado and put one over on the Dutchman. The fact that he had on a red sweater was the barest coincidence. Having observed the brick to be accurately pursuing its proper trajectory he had ducked back round the corner again and continued upon his way rejoicing. He had not even noticed Tony Mathusek, who, having accidentally found himself in the midst of the mêlée, had started to beat a retreat the instant of the crash, and had run plump into the arms of Officer Delany of the Second. Unfortunately Tony too was wearing a red sweater.

"I've got you, you young devil!" exulted Delany. "Here's one of 'em, Froelich!"

"Dot's him! It was a feller mit a red sweater! Dot's the vun who done it!" shrieked the butcher. "I vill make a gomblaint against him!"

"Come along, you! Quit yer kickin'!" ordered the cop, twisting Tony's thin arm until he writhed. "You'll identify him, Froelich?"

"Sure! Didn't I see him mit my eyes? He's vun of dem rascals vot drives all mine gustomers avay mit deir yelling and screaming. You fix it for me, Bill."

"That's all right," the officer assured him. "I'll fix him good, I will! It's the reformatory for him. Or, say, you can make a complaint for malicious mischief."

"Sure! Dot's it! Malicious mischief!" assented the not over-intelligent tradesman. "Ve'll get rid of him for good, eh?"

"Sure," assented Delany. "Come along, you!"

Tony Mathusek lifted a white face drawn with agony from his tortured arm.

"Say, mister, you got the wrong feller! I didn't break the window. I was just comin' from the house—"

"Aw, shut up!" sneered Delany. "Tell that to the judge!"

"Y' ain't goin' to take me to jail?" wailed Tony. "I wasn't with them boys. I don't belong to that gang."

"Oh, so you belong to a gang, do ye? Well, we don't want no gangsters round here!" cried the officer with adroit if unscrupulous sophistry. "Come along now, and keep quiet or it'll be the worse for ye."

"Can't I tell my mother? She'll be lookin' for me. She's an old lady."

"Tell nuthin'. You come along!"

Tony saw all hope fade. He hadn't a chance—even to go to a decent jail! He had heard all about the horrors of the reformatory. They wouldn't even let your people visit you on Sundays! And his mother would think he was run over or murdered. She would go crazy with worry. He didn't mind on his own account, but his mother— He loved the old widowed mother who worked her fingers off to send him to school. And he was the only one left, now that Peter had been killed in the war. It was too much. With a sudden twist he tore out of his coat and dashed blindly down the street. As well might a rabbit hope to escape the claws of a wildcat. In three bounds Delany had him again, choking him until the world turned black.

But this is not a story about police brutality, for most cops are not brutal. Delany was an old-timer who believed in rough methods. He belonged, happily, to a fast-vanishing system more in harmony with the middle ages than with our present enlightened form of municipal government. He remained what he was for the reason that farther up in the official hierarchy there were others who looked to him, when it was desirable, to deliver the goods—not necessarily cash—but to stand with the bunch. These in turn were obligated on occasion, through self-interest or mistaken loyalty to friend or party, to overlook trifling irregularities, to use various sorts of pressure, or to forget what they were asked to forget. There was a far-reaching web of complicated relationships—official, political, matrimonial, commercial and otherwise—which had a very practical effect upon the performance of theoretical duty.

Delany was neither an idealist nor a philosopher. He was an empiricist, with a touch of pragmatism—though he did not know it. He was "a practical man." Even reform administrations have been known to advocate a liberal enforcement of the laws. Can you blame Delany for being practical when others so much greater than he have prided themselves upon the same attribute of practicality? There were of course a lot of things he simply had to do or get out of the force; at any rate, had he not done them his life would have been intolerable. These consisted in part of being deaf, dumb and blind when he was told to be so—a comparatively easy matter. But there were other things that he had to do, as a matter of fact, to show that he was all right, which were not only more difficult, but expensive, and at times dangerous.

He had never been called upon to swear away an innocent man's liberty, but more than once he had had to stand for a frame-up against a guilty one. According to his cop-psychology, if his side partner saw something it was practically the same as if he had seen it himself. That phantasmagorical scintilla of evidence needed to bolster up a weak or doubtful case could always be counted on if Delany was the officer who had made the arrest. None of his cases were ever thrown out of court for lack of evidence, but then, Delany never arrested anybody who wasn't guilty!

Of course he had to "give up" at intervals, depending on what administration was in power, who his immediate superior was, and what precinct he was attached to, but he was not a regular grafter by any means. He was an occasional one merely; when he had to be. He did not consider that he was being grafted on when expected to contribute to chowders, picnics, benevolent associations, defense funds or wedding presents for high police officials. Neither did he think that he was taking graft because he amicably permitted Froelich to leave a fourteen-pound rib roast every Saturday night at his brother-in-law's flat. In the same way he regarded the bills slipped him by Grabinsky, the bondsman, as well-earned commissions, and saw no reason why the civilian clothes he ordered at the store shouldn't be paid for by some mysterious friendly person—identity unknown—but shrewdly suspected to be Mr. Joseph Simpkins, Mr. Hogan's runner. Weren't there to be any cakes and ale in New York simply because a highbrow happened to be mayor? Were human kindness, good nature and generosity all dead? Would he have taken a ten-dollar bill—or even a hundred-dollar one—from Simpkins when he was going to be a witness in one of Hogan's cases? Not on your life! He wasn't no crook, he wasn't! He didn't have to be. He was just a cog in an immense wheel of crookedness. When the wheel came down on his cog he automatically did his part.

I perceive that the police are engaging too much of our attention. But it is necessary to explain why Delany was so ready to arrest Tony Mathusek, and why as he dragged him into the station house he beckoned to Mr. Joey Simpkins, who was loitering outside in front of the deputy sheriff's office, and whispered behind his hand, "All right. I've got one for you!"

Then the machine began to work as automatically as a cash register. Tony was arraigned at the bar, and, having given his age as sixteen years and five days, charged with the "malicious destruction of property, to wit, a plate-glass window of one Karl Froelich, of the value of one hundred and fifty dollars." Mr. Joey Simpkins had shouldered his way through the smelly push and taken his stand beside the bewildered and half-fainting boy.

"It's all right, kid. Leave it to me," he said, encircling him with a protecting arm. Then to the clerk: "Pleads not guilty."

The magistrate glanced over the complaint, in which Delany, to save Froelich trouble, had sworn that he had seen Tony throw the brick. Hadn't the butcher said he'd seen him? Besides, that let the Dutchman out of a possible suit for false arrest. Then the magistrate looked down at the cop himself.

"Do you know this boy?" he asked sharply.

"Sure, Yerroner. He's a gangster. Admitted it to me on the way over."

"Are you really over sixteen?" suddenly demanded the judge, who knew and distrusted Delany, having repeatedly stated in open court that he wouldn't hang a yellow dog on his testimony. The underfed, undersized boy did not look more than fourteen.

"Yes, sir," said Tony. "I was sixteen last week."

"Got anybody to defend you?"

Tony looked at Simpkins inquiringly. He seemed a very kind gentleman.

"Mr. Hogan's case, judge," answered Joey. "Please make the bail as low as you can."

Now this judge was a political accident, having been pitchforked into office by the providence that sometimes watches over sailors, drunks and third parties. Moreover, in spite of being a reformer he was nobody's fool, and when the other reformers who were fools got promptly fired out of office he had been reappointed by a supposedly crooked boss simply because, as the boss said, he had made a hell of a good judge and they needed somebody with brains here and there to throw a front. Incidentally, he had a swell cousin on Fifth Avenue who had invited the boss and his wife to dinner, by reason of which the soreheads who lost out went round asking what kind of a note it was when a silk-stocking crook could buy a nine-thousand-dollar job for a fifty-dollar dinner. Anyhow, he was clean and clean-looking, kindly, humorous and wise above his years—which were thirty-one. And Tony looked to him like a poor runt, Simpkins and Delany were both rascals, Froelich wasn't in court, and he sensed a nigger somewhere. He would have turned Tony out on the run had he had any excuse. He hadn't, but he tried.

"Would you like an immediate hearing?" he asked Tony in an encouraging tone.

"Mr. Hogan can't be here until to-morrow morning," interposed Simpkins. "Besides, we shall want to produce witnesses. Make it to-morrow afternoon, judge."

Judge Harrison leaned forward.

"Are you sure you wouldn't prefer to have the hearing now?" he inquired with a smile at the trembling boy.

"Well, I want to get Froelich here—if you're going to proceed now," spoke up Delany. "And I'd like to look up this defendant's record at headquarters."

Tony quailed. He feared and distrusted everybody, except the kind Mr. Simpkins. He suspected that smooth judge of trying to railroad him.

"No! No!" he whispered to the lawyer. "I want my mother should be here; and the janitor, he knows I was in my house. The rabbi, he will give me a good character."

The judge heard and shrugged his bombazine-covered shoulders. It was no use. The children of darkness were wiser in their generation than the children of light.

"Five hundred dollars bail," he remarked shortly. "Officer, have your witnesses ready to proceed to-morrow afternoon at two o'clock."

"Mr. Tutt," said Tutt with a depressed manner as he watched Willie remove the screen and drag out the old gate-leg table for the firm's daily five o'clock tea and conference in the senior partner's office, "if a man called you a shyster what would you do about it?"

The elder lawyer sucked meditatively on the fag end of his stogy before replying.

"Why not sue him?" Mr. Tutt inquired.

"But suppose he didn't have any money?" replied Tutt disgustedly.

"Then why not have him arrested?" continued Mr. Tutt. "It's libelous *per se* to call a lawyer a shyster."

"Even if he is one," supplemented Miss Minerva Wiggin ironically, as she removed her paper cuffs preparatory to lighting the alcohol lamp under the teakettle. "The greater the truth the greater the libel, you know!"

"And what do you mean by that?" sharply rejoined Tutt. "You don't—"

"No," replied the managing clerk of Tutt & Tutt. "I don't! Of course not! And frankly, I don't know what a shyster is."

"Neither do I," admitted Tutt. "But it sounds opprobrious. Still, that is a rather dangerous test. You remember that colored client of ours who wanted us to bring an action against somebody for calling him an Ethiopian!"

"There's nothing dishonorable in being an Ethiopian," asserted Miss Wiggin.

"A shyster," said Mr. Tutt, reading from the Century Dictionary, "is defined as 'one who does business trickily; a person without professional honor; used chiefly of lawyers.'"

"Well?" snapped Tutt.

"Well?" echoed Miss Wiggin.

"H'm! Well!" concluded Mr. Tutt.

"I nominate for the first pedestal in our Hall of Legal Ill Fame—Raphael B. Hogan," announced Tutt, complacently disregarding all innuendoes.

"But he's a very elegant and gentlemanly person," objected Miss Wiggin as she warmed the cups. "My idea of a shyster is a down-at-the-heels, unshaved and generally disreputable-looking police-court lawyer—preferably with a red nose—who murders the English language—and who makes his living by preying upon the ignorant and helpless."

"Like Finklestein?" suggested Tutt.

"Exactly!" agreed Miss Wiggin. "Like Finklestein."

"He's one of the most honorable men I know!" protested Mr. Tutt. "My dear Minerva, you are making the great mistake—common, I confess, to a large number of people—of associating dirt and crime. Now dirt may breed crime, but crime doesn't necessarily breed dirt."

"You don't have to be shabby to prey upon the ignorant and helpless," argued Tutt. "Some of our most prosperous brethren are the worst sharks out of Sing Sing."

"That is true!" she admitted, "but tell it not in Gath!"

"A shyster," began Mr. Tutt, unsuccessfully applying a forced draft to his stogy and then throwing it away, "bears about the same relation to an honest lawyer as a cad does to a gentleman. The fact that he's well dressed, belongs to a good club and has his name in the Social Register doesn't affect the situation. Clothes don't make men; they only make opportunities."

"But why is it," persisted Miss Wiggin, "that we invariably associate the idea of crime with that of 'poverty, hunger and dirt'?"

"That is easy to explain," asserted Mr. Tutt. "The criminal law originally dealt only with crimes of violence—such as murder, rape and assault. In the old days people didn't have any property in the modern sense—except their land, their cattle or their weapons. They had no bonds or stock or bank accounts. Now it is of course true that rough, ignorant people are much more prone to violence of speech and action than those of gentle breeding, and hence most of our crimes of violence are committed by those whose lives are those of squalor. But"—and here Mr. Tutt's voice rose indignantly—"our greatest mistake is to assume that crimes of violence are the most dangerous to the state, for they are not. They cause greater disturbance and perhaps more momentary inconvenience, but they do not usually evince much moral turpitude. After all, it does no great harm if one man punches another in the head, or even in a fit of anger sticks a dagger in him. The police can easily handle all that. The real danger to the community lies in the crimes of duplicity—the cheats, frauds, false pretenses, tricks and devices, flimflams—practised most successfully by well-dressed gentlemanly crooks of polished manners."

By this time the kettle was boiling cheerfully, quite as if no such thing as criminal law existed at all, and Miss Wiggin began to make the tea.

"All the same," she ruminated, "people—particularly very poor people—are often driven to crime by necessity."

"It's Nature's first law," contributed Tutt brightly.

Mr. Tutt uttered a snort of disgust.

"It may be Nature's first law, but it's about the weakest defense a guilty man can offer. 'I couldn't help myself' has always been the excuse for helping oneself!"

"Rather good—that!" approved Miss Wiggin. "Can you do it again?"

"The victim of circumstances is inevitably one who has made a victim of someone else," blandly went on Mr. Tutt without hesitation.

"Ting-a-ling! Right on the bell!" she laughed.

"It's true!" he assured her seriously. "There are two defenses that are played out—necessity and instigation. They've never been any good since the Almighty overruled Adam's plea in confession and avoidance that a certain female co-defendant took advantage of his hungry innocence and put him up to it."

"No one could respect a man who tried to hide behind a woman's skirts!" commented Tutt.

"Are you referring to Adam?" inquired his partner. "Anyhow, come to think of it, the maxim is not that 'Necessity is the first law of Nature,' but that 'Necessity knows no law.'"

"I'll bet you—" began Tutt. Then he paused, recalling a certain celebrated wager which he had lost to Mr. Tutt upon the question of who cut Samson's hair. "I bet you don't know who said it!" he concluded lamely.

"If I recall correctly," ruminated Mr. Tutt, "Shakspere says in 'Julius Caesar' that 'Nature must obey necessity'; while Rabelais says 'Necessity has no law'; but the quotation we familiarly use is 'Necessity knows no law except to conquer,' which is from Publilius Syrus."

"From who?" cried Tutt in ungrammatical surprise.

"Never mind!" soothed Miss Wiggin. "Anyway, it wasn't Raphael B. Hogan."

"Who certainly completely satisfies your definition so far as preying upon the ignorant and helpless is concerned," said Mr. Tutt. "That man is a human hyena—worse than a highwayman."

"Yet he's a swell dresser," interjected Tutt. "Owns his house and lives in amity with his wife."

"Doubtless he's a loyal husband and a devoted father," agreed Mr. Tutt. "But so, very likely, is the hyena. Certainly Hogan hasn't got the excuse of necessity for doing what he does."

"Don't you suppose he has to give up good and plenty to somebody?" demanded Tutt. "Cops and prison keepers and bondsmen and under sheriffs, and all kinds of crooked petty officials. I should worry!"

9

*"Great fleas have little fleas upon their backs to bite 'em,
And little fleas have lesser fleas, and so ad infinitum,"*
quoted Miss Wiggin reminiscently.

"A flea has to be a flea," continued Tutt. "He, or it, can't be anything else, but Hogan doesn't have to be a lawyer. He could be an honest man if he chose."

"He? Not on your life! He couldn't be honest if he tried!" roared Mr. Tutt. "He's just a carnivorous animal! A man eater! They talk about scratching a Russian and finding a Tartar; I'd hate to scratch some of our legal brethren."

"So would I!" assented Tutt. "I guess you're right, Mr. Tutt. Christianity and the Golden Rule are all right in the upper social circles, but off Fifth Avenue there's the same sort of struggle for existence that goes on in the animal world. A man may be all sweetness and light to his wife and children and go to church on Sundays; he may even play pretty fair with his own gang; but outside of his home and social circle he's a ravening wolf; at least Raphael B. Hogan is!"

The subject of the foregoing entirely accidental conversation was at that moment standing contemplatively in his office window smoking an excellent cigar preparatory to returning to the bosom of his family. Raphael B. Hogan believed in taking life easily. He was accustomed to say that outside office hours his time belonged to his wife and children; and several times a week he made it his habit on the way home to supper to stop at the florist's or the toy shop and bear away with him inexpensive tokens of his love and affection. On the desk behind him, over which in the course of each month passed a lot of very tainted money, stood a large photograph of Mrs. Hogan, and another of the three little Hogans in ornamented silver frames, and his face would soften tenderly at the sight of their self-conscious faces, even at a moment when he might be relieving a widowed seamstress of her entire savings-bank account. After five o'clock this hyena purred at his wife and licked his cubs; the rest of the time he knew no mercy.

But he concealed his cruelty and his avarice under a mask of benignity. He was fat, jolly and sympathetic, and his smile was the smile of a warm-hearted humanitarian. The milk of human kindness oozed from his every pore. In fact, he was always grumbling about the amount of work he had to do for nothing. He was a genial, generous host; unostentatiously conspicuous in the local religious life of his denomination; in court a model of obsequious urbanity, deferential to the judges before whom he appeared and courteous to all with whom he was thrown in contact. A good-natured, easy-going, simple-minded fat man; deliberate, slow of speech, well-meaning, with honesty sticking out all over him, you would have said; one in whom the widow and the orphan would have found a staunch protector and an unselfish friend. And now, having thus subtly connoted the character of our villain, let us proceed with our narrative.

The telephone buzzed on the wall set beside him.

"That you, chief?" came the voice of Simpkins.

"Yep."

"Got one off Delany."

"What is it?"

"Kid smashed a window—malicious mischief. Held for examination tomorrow at two. Five hundred bail."

"Any sugar?"

"Don't know. Says his father's dead and mother earns seventeen a week in a sweatshop and sends him to school. Got some insurance. I'm going right round there now."

"Well," replied Hogan, "don't scare her by taking too much off her at first. I suppose there's evidence to hold him?"

"Sure. Delany says he saw it."

"All right. But go easy! Good night."

"Leave that to me, chief!" assured Simpkins. "See you to-morrow."

It will be observed that in this professional interchange nothing at all was said regarding the possibility of establishing Tony's innocence, but that on the contrary Mr. Simpkins' mind was concentrated upon his mother's ability to pay. This was the only really important consideration to either of them. But Hogan did not worry, because he knew that Simpkins would skilfully entangle Mrs. Mathusek in such a web of apprehension that rather than face her fears she would if necessary go out and steal the money. So Mr. Raphael B. Hogan hung up the receiver and with his heart full of gentle sympathy for all mankind walked slowly home, pausing to get some roses for Mrs. Hogan and to buy a box for Daddy Long Legs at the Strand, for whenever he got a new case he always made it the occasion for a family party, and he wanted the children to benefit by passing an evening under the sweet influence of Miss Pickford.

Now just at the moment that his employer was buying the roses Mr. Simpkins entered the apartment of Mrs. Mathusek and informed her of Tony's arrest and incarceration. He was very sympathetic about it, very gentle, this dapper little man with the pale gray eyes and inquisitive, tapirlike nose; and after the first moment of shock Mrs. Mathusek took courage and begged the gentleman to sit down. There are always two vultures hanging over the poor—death and the law; but of the two the law is the lesser evil. The former is a calamity; the latter is a misfortune. The one is final, hopeless, irretrievable; from the other there may perhaps be an escape. She knew Tony was a good boy; was sure his arrest was a mistake, and that when the judge heard the evidence he would let Tony go. Life had dealt hardly with her and made her an old woman at thirty-four, really old, not only in body but in spirit, just as in the middle ages the rigor of existence made even kings old at thirty-five. What do the rich know of age? The women of the poor have a day of spring, a year or two of summer, and a lifetime of autumn and winter.

Mrs. Mathusek distrusted the law and lawyers in the abstract, but Mr. Simpkins' appearance was so reassuring that he almost counteracted in her mind the distress of Tony's misfortune. He was clearly a gentleman, and she had a reverential regard for the gentry. What gentlefolk said was to be accepted as true. In addition this particular gentleman was learned in the law and skilled in getting unfortunate people out of trouble. Now, though Mr. Simpkins possessed undoubtedly this latter qualification, it was also true that he was equally skilled in getting people into it. If he ultimately doubled their joys and halved their sorrows he inevitably first doubled their sorrows and halved their savings. Like the witch in Macbeth: "Double, double toil and trouble." His aims were childishly simple: First, to find out how much money his victim had, and then to get it.

His methods were no more complicated than his aims and had weathered the test of generations of experience. So:

"Of course Tony must be bailed out," he said gently. "You don't want him to spend the night in jail."

"Jail! Oh, no! How much is the bail?" cried Tony's mother.

"Only five hundred dollars." His pale gray eyes were watching her for the slightest sign of suspicion.

"Five hundred dollars! Eoi! Eoi! It is a fortune! Where can I get five hundred dollars?" She burst into tears. "I have saved only one hundred and sixty!"

Mr. Simpkins pursed his lips. Then there was nothing for it! He reached for his hat. Mrs. Mathusek wrung her hands. Couldn't the gentleman go bail for Tony? He was such a dear, kind, good gentleman! She searched his face hungrily. Mr. Simpkins falteringly admitted that he did not possess five hundred dollars.

"But—" he hesitated.

"Yes!"

"But—" she echoed, seizing his sleeve and dragging him back.

Mr. Simpkins thought that they could hire somebody to go bail; no, in that case there would be no money to pay the great lawyer whom they must at once engage to defend her son—Mr. Hogan, one who had the pull and called all the judges by their first names. He would not usually go into court for less than five hundred dollars, but Mr. Simpkins said he would explain the circumstances to him and could almost promise Mrs. Mathusek that he would persuade him to do it this once for one hundred and fifty. So well did he act his part that Tony's mother had to force him to take the money, which she unsewed from inside the ticking of her mattress. Then he conducted her to the station house to show her how comfortable Tony really was and how much better it was to let him stay in jail one night and make sure of his being turned out the next afternoon by giving the money to Mr. Hogan, than to use it for getting bail for him and leave him lawyerless and at the mercy of his accusers. When Mrs. Mathusek saw the cell Tony was in she became even more frightened than she had been at first. But by that time she had already given the money to Simpkins.

Second thoughts are ofttimes best. Most crooks are eventually caught through their having, from long immunity, grown careless and yielded to impulse. Once he had signed the complaint in which he swore that he had seen Tony throw the brick, Delany had undergone a change of heart. Being an experienced policeman he was sensitive to official atmosphere, and he had developed a hunch that Judge Harrison was leery of the case. The more he thought of it the less he liked the way the son-of-a-gun had acted, the way he'd tried to get Mathusek to ask for an immediate hearing. Why had he ever been such a fool as to sign the complaint himself? It had been ridiculous—just because he was mad at the boy for trying to get away and wanted to make things easy for Froelich. If he went on the stand the next afternoon he'd have to make up all sorts of fancy details, and Hogan would have his skin neatly tacked to the barn doors for keeps. Thereafter, no matter what happened, he'd never be able to change his testimony. After all, it would be easy enough to abandon the charge at the present point. It was a genuine case of cold feet. He scented trouble. He wanted to renig while the renigging was good. What in hell had Froelich ever done for him, anyhow? A few measly pieces of roast!

When Hogan returned home that evening with the little Hogans from the movies he found the cop waiting for him outside his door.

"Look here," Delany whispered, "I'm going to can this here Mathusek window case. I'm going to fall down flat on my identification and give you a walkout. So go easy on me—and sort of help me along, see?"

"The hell you are!" retorted Hogan indignantly. "Then where do I come in, eh? Why don't you come through?"

"But I've got him wrong!" pleaded Delany. "You don't want me to put my neck in a sling, do you, so as you can make a few dollars? Look at all the money I've sent your way. Have a heart, Rafe!"

"Bull!" sneered the Honorable Rafe. "A man's gotta live! You saw him do it! You've sworn to it, haven't you?"

"I made a mistake."

"How'll that sound to the commissioner? An' to Judge Harrison? No, no! Nothin' doin'! If you start anything like that I'll roast the life out of you!"

Delany spat as near Hogan's foot as he elegantly could.

"You're a hell of a feller, you are!" he growled, and turned his back on him as upon Satan.

The brick that Terry McGurk hurled as a matter of principle through Froelich's window produced almost as momentous consequences as the want of the horseshoe nail did in Franklin's famous maxim. It is the unknown element in every transaction that makes for danger.

The morning after the catastrophe Mr. Froelich promptly made application to the casualty company with which he had insured his window for reimbursement for his damage. Just as promptly the company's lawyer appeared at the butcher shop and ascertained that the miscreant who had done the foul deed had been arrested and was to be brought into court that afternoon. This lawyer, whose salary depended indirectly upon the success which attended his efforts to secure the conviction and punishment of those who had cost his company money, immediately camped upon the trails of both Froelich and Delany. It was up to them, he said, to have the doer of wanton mischief sent away. If they didn't cooperate he would most certainly ascertain why. Now insurance companies are powerful corporations. They can do favors, and contrariwise they can make trouble, and Lawyer Asche was hot under the collar about that window. Had he ever heard of the place he would have likened it to the destruction of Coucy-le-Château by the Huns.

This, for Delany, put an entirely new aspect upon the affair. It was one thing to ditch a case and another to run up against Nathan Asche. He had sworn to the complaint and if he didn't make good on the witness stand Asche would get his hide. Then he bethought him that if only Froelich was sufficiently emphatic in his testimony a little uncertainty on his own part might be excused.

In the meantime, however, two things had happened to curdle Froelich's enthusiasm. First, his claim against the Tornado Casualty Company had been approved, and second, he had been informed on credible authority that they had got the wrong boy. Now he had sincerely thought that he had seen Tony throw the brick—he had certainly seen a boy in a red sweater do something—but he realized also that he had been excited and more or less bewildered at the time; and his informant—Mrs. Sussman, the wife of the cigar dealer—alleged positively that it had been thrown by a strange kid who appeared suddenly from round the corner and as suddenly ran away in the direction whence he had come.

Froelich perceived that he had probably been mistaken, and being relatively honest—and being also about to get his money—and not wishing to bear false witness, particularly if he might later be sued for false imprisonment, he decided to duck and pass the buck to Delany, who was definitely committed. He was shrewd enough, however, not to give his real reason to the policeman, but put it on the ground of being so confused that he couldn't remember. This left Delany responsible for everything.

"But you said that that was the feller!" argued the cop, who had gone to urge Froelich to assume the onus of the charge. "And now you want to leave me holdin' the bag!"

"Vell, you said yourself you seen him, didn't you?" replied the German. "An' you svore to it. I didn't svear to noddings."

"Aw, you!" roared the enraged cop, and hastened to interview Mr. Asche.

Aping a broad humanitarianism he suggested to Asche that if Mrs. Mathusek would pay for the window they could afford to let up on the boy. He did it so ingeniously that he got Asche to go round there, only to find that she had no money, all given to Simpkins. Gee, what a mix-up!

It is quite possible that even under these circumstances Delany might still have availed himself of what in law is called a *locus poenitentiae* had it not been that the mix-up was rendered still more mixed by the surreptitious appearance in the case of Mr. Michael McGurk, the father of the actual brick artist, who had learned that the cop was getting wabbly and was entertaining the preposterous possibility of withdrawing the charge against the innocent Mathusek, to the imminent danger of his own offspring. In no uncertain terms the saloon keeper intimated to the now embarrassed guardian of the public peace that if he pulled anything like that he would have him thrown off the force, to say nothing of other and darker possibilities connected with the morgue. All of which gave Delany decided pause.

Hogan, for his own reasons, had meanwhile reached an independent conclusion as to how he could circumvent Delany's contemplated treachery. If, he decided, the cop should go back on his identification of the criminal he foresaw Tony's discharge in the magistrate's court, and no more money. The only sure way, therefore, to prevent Tony's escape would be by not giving Delany the chance to change his testimony; and by waiving examination before the magistrate and consenting voluntarily to having his client held for the action of the grand jury, in which event Tony would be sent to the Tombs and there would be plenty of time for Simpkins to get an assignment of Mrs. Mathusek's insurance money before the grand jury kicked out the case. This also had the additional advantage of preventing any funny business on the part of Judge Harrison.

Delany was still undecided what he was going to do when the case was called at two o'clock. It is conceivable that he might still have tried to rectify his error by telling something near the truth, in spite of Hogan, Asche and McGurk, but the opportunity was denied him.

At two o'clock Tony, a mere chip tossed aimlessly hither and yon by eddies and cross currents, the only person in this melodrama of motive whose interests were not being considered by anybody, was arraigned at the bar and, without being consulted in the matter, heard Mr. Hogan, the fat, kindly lawyer whom his mother had retained to defend him, tell the judge that they were going to waive examination and consent to be held for the action of the grand jury.

"You see how it is, judge," Hogan simpered. "You'd have no choice but to hold my client on the officer's testimony. The easiest way is to waive examination and let the grand jury throw the case out of the window!"

Delany heard this announcement with intense relief, for it let him out. It would relieve him from the dangerous necessity of testifying before Judge Harrison and he could later spill the case before the grand jury when called before that august body. Moreover, he could tip off the district attorney in charge of the indictment bureau that the case was a lemon, and the latter would probably throw it out on his own motion. The D.A.'s office didn't want any more rotten cases to prosecute than it could help. It seemed his one best bet, the only way to get his feet out of the flypaper. What a mess for a few pieces of rotten beef!

"You understand what is being done, do you?" inquired the keen-faced judge sharply. "You understand this means that unless you give bail you will have to stay in jail until the grand jury dismisses the case or finds an indictment against you?"

Underneath the cornice of the judge's dais Hogan patted his arm, and Tony, glancing for encouragement at the big friendly face above him, whispered "Yes."

So Tony went to the Tombs and was lodged in a cell next door to Soko the Monk, who had nearly beaten a Chinaman to death with a pair of brass knuckles, from whom he learned much that was exciting if not edifying.

Now, as Delany was wont to say for years thereafter, that damn Mathusek case just went bad on him. He had believed that in the comparative secrecy of the inquisitorial chamber he could easily pretend that he had originally made an honest mistake and was no longer positive of the defendant's identity, in which case when the grand jury threw out the case nobody would ever know the reason and no chickens would come home to roost on him.

But when the cop visited the office of Deputy Assistant District Attorney Caput Magnus the next morning, to inform him that this here window-breaking case was a Messina, he found Mr. Nathan Asche already solidly there present, engaged in advising Mr. Magnus most emphatically to the exact contrary.

Indeed the attorney was rhetorical in his insistence that this destruction of the property of law-abiding taxpayers must stop.

Mr. Asche was not a party to be trifled with. He was a rectangular person whom nothing could budge, and his very rectangularity bespoke his stubborn rectitude. His shoulders were massive and square, his chin and mouth were square, his burnsides were square cut, and he had a square head and wore a square-topped derby. He looked like the family portrait of Uncle Amos Hardscrabble. When he sat down he remained until he had said his say. It was a misfortunate meeting for Delany, for Asche nailed him upon the spot and made him repeat to Caput Magnus the story of how he had seen Tony throw the brick and then, for some fool reason, not being satisfied to let it go at that, he insisted on calling in a stenographer and having Delany swear to the yarn in affidavit form! This entirely spoiled any chance the policeman might otherwise have had of changing his testimony. He now had no choice but to go on and swear the case through before the grand jury—which he did.

Even so, that distinguished body of twenty-three representative citizens was not disposed to take the matter very seriously. Having heard what Delany had to say—and he made it good and strong under the circumstances—several of them remarked disgustedly that they did not understand why the district attorney saw fit to waste their valuable time with trivial cases of that sort. Boys would play ball and boys would throw balls round; if not balls, then stones. They were about to dismiss by an almost unanimous vote, when the case went bad again. The foreman, a distinguished person in braided broadcloth, rose and announced that he was very much interested to learn their views upon this subject as he was the president of a casualty company, and he wished them to understand that thousands—if not hundreds of thousands—of dollars' worth of plate-glass windows were wantonly broken by young toughs, every year, for which his and other insurance companies had to recoup the owners. In fact, he alleged heatedly, window breaking was a sign of peculiar viciousness. Incipient criminals usually started their infamous careers that way; you could read that in any book on penology. An example ought to be made. He'd bet this feller who threw the brick was a gangster.

So his twenty-two fellow grand jurymen politely permitted him to recall Officer Delany and ask him: "Say, officer, isn't it a fact—just tell us frankly now—if this feller Mathusek isn't a gangster?"

"Sure, he's a gangster. He was blowin' about it to me after I arrested him," swore Delany without hesitation.

The foreman swept the circle with a triumphant eye.

"What'd I tell you?" he demanded. "All in favor of indicting said Tony Mathusek for malicious destruction of property signify in the usual manner. Cont'riminded? It's a vote. Ring the bell, Simmons, and bring on the next case."

So Tony was indicted by the People of the State of New York for a felony, and a learned judge of the General Sessions set his bail at fifteen hundred dollars; and Hogan had his victim where he wanted him and where he could keep him until he had bled his mother white of all she had or might ever hope to have in this world.

Everybody was satisfied—Hogan, Simpkins, Asche, McGurk, even Delany, because the fleas upon his back were satisfied and he was planning ultimately to get rid of the whole damn tangle by having the indictment quietly dismissed when nobody was looking, by his friend O'Brien, to whom the case had been sent for trial. And everything being as it should be, and Tony being locked safely up in a cell, Mr. Joey Simpkins set himself to the task of extorting three hundred and fifty dollars more from Mrs. Mathusek upon the plea that the great Mr. Hogan could not possibly conduct the case before a jury for less.

Now the relations of Mr. Assistant District Attorney O'Brien and the Hon. Raphael B. Hogan were distinctly friendly. At any rate, whenever Mr. Hogan asked for an adjournment in Mr. O'Brien's court he usually got it without conspicuous difficulty, and that is what occurred on the five several occasions that the case of The People versus Antonio Mathusek came up on the trial calendar during the month following Tony's incarceration, on each of which Mr. Hogan with unctuous suavity rose and humbly requested that the case be put over at his client's earnest request in order that counsel might have adequate time in which to subpoena witnesses and prepare for a defense.

And each day Simpkins, who now assumed a threatening and fearsome demeanor toward Mrs. Mathusek, visited the heartsick woman in her flat and told her that Tony could and would rot in the Tombs until such time as she procured three hundred and fifty dollars. The first week she assigned her life-insurance money; the second she pawned the furniture; until at last she owed Hogan only sixty-five dollars. At intervals Hogan told Tony that he was trying to force the district attorney to try the case, but that the latter was insisting on delay.

In point of fact, O'Brien had never looked at the papers, much less made any effort to prepare the case; if he had he would have found that there was no case at all. And Delany's mind became at peace because he perceived that at the proper psychological moment he could go to O'Brien and whisper: "Say, Mr. O'Brien, that Mathusek case. It's a turn-out! Better recommend it for dismissal," and O'Brien would do so for the simple reason that he never did any more work than he was actually compelled to do.

But as chance would have it, three times out of the five, Mr. Ephraim Tutt happened to be in court when Mr. Hogan rose and made his request for an adjournment; and he remembered it because the offense charged was such an odd one—breaking a window.

Delany's simple plan was again defeated by Nemesis, who pursued him in the shape of the rectangular Mr. Asche, and who shouldered himself into O'Brien's office during the fifth week of Tony's imprisonment and wanted to know why in hell he didn't try that Mathusek case and get rid of it. The assistant district attorney had just been called down by his official boss and being still sore was glad of a chance to take it out on someone else.

"D'you think I've nothin' better to do than try your damned old window-busting cases?" he sneered. "Who ever had the idea of indicting a boy for that sort of thing, anyhow?"

"That is no way to talk," answered Mr. Asche with firmness. "You're paid to prosecute whatever cases are sent to you. This is one of 'em. There's been too much delay. Our president will be annoyed."

"Oh, he will, will he?" retorted O'Brien, nevertheless, coming to the instant decision that he had best find some other excuse than mere disinclination. "If he gets too shirty I'll tell him the case came in here without any preparation and being in the nature of a private prosecution we've been waiting for you to earn your fee. How'll you like that, eh?"

Mr. Asche became discolored.

"H'm!" he replied softly. "So that is it, is it? You won't have that excuse very long, even if you could get away with it now. I'll have a trial brief and affidavits from all the witnesses ready for you in forty-eight hours."

"All right, old top!" nodded O'Brien carelessly. "We always strive to please!"

So Mr. Asche got busy, while the very same day Mr. Hogan asked for and obtained another adjournment.

Some people resemble animals; others have a geometrical aspect. In each class the similarity tends to indicate character. The fox-faced man is apt to be sly, the triangular man is likely to be a lump. So Mr. Asche, being rectilinear, was on the square; just as Mr. Hogan, being soft and round, was slippery and hard to hold. Three days passed, during which Mrs. Mathusek grew haggard and desperate. She was saving at the rate of two dollars a day, and at that rate she would be able to buy Tony a trial in five weeks more. She had exhausted her possibilities as a borrower. The indictment slept in O'Brien's tin file. Nobody but Tony, his mother and Hogan remembered that there was any such case, except Mr. Asche, who one afternoon appeared unexpectedly in the offices of Tutt & Tutt, the senior partner of which celebrated law firm happened to be advisory counsel to the Tornado Casualty Company.

"I just want you to look at these papers, Mr. Tutt," Mr. Asche said, and his jaw looked squarer than ever.

Mr. Tutt was reclining as usual in his swivel chair, his feet crossed upon the top of his ancient mahogany desk.

"Take a stog!" he remarked without getting up, and indicating with the toe of one Congress-booted foot the box which lay open adjacent to the Code of Criminal Procedure. "What's your misery?"

"Hell's at work!" returned Mr. Asche, solemnly handing over a sheaf of affidavits. "I never smoke."

Mr. Tutt somewhat reluctantly altered his position from the horizontal to the vertical and reached for a fresh stogy. Then his eye caught the name of Raphael B. Hogan.

"What the devil is this?" he cried.

"It's the devil himself!" answered Mr. Asche with sudden vehemence.

"Tutt, Tutt! Come in here!" shouted the head of the firm. "Mine enemy hath been delivered into mine hands!"

"Hey? What?" inquired Tutt, popping across the threshold. "Who—I mean—"

"Raphael B. Hogan!"

"The devil!" ejaculated Tutt.

"You've said it!" declared Mr. Asche devoutly.

That evening under cover of darkness Mr. Ephraim Tutt descended from a dilapidated taxi at the corner adjacent to Froelich's butcher shop, and several hours later was whisked uptown again to the brownstone dwelling occupied by the Hon. Simeon Watkins, the venerable white-haired judge then presiding in Part I of the General Sessions, where he remained until what may be described either as a very late or a very early hour, and where during the final period of his intercourse he and that distinguished member of the judiciary emptied an ancient bottle containing a sparkling rose-colored liquid of great artistic beauty.

Then Mr. Tutt returned to his own library at the house on Twenty-third Street and paced up and down before the antiquated open grate, inhaling quantities of what Mr. Bonnie Doon irreverently called "hay smoke," and pondering deeply upon the evils that men do to one another, until the dawn peered through the windows and he bethought him of the all-night lunch stand round the corner on Tenth Avenue, and there sought refreshment.

"Salvatore," he remarked to the smiling son of the olive groves who tended that bar of innocence, "the worst crook in the world is the man who does evil for mere money."

"*Si, Signor Tutti,*" answered Salvatore with Latin perspicacity. "You gotta one, eh? You giva him hell?"

"*Si! Si!*" replied Mr. Tutt cheerily. "Even so! And of a truth, moreover! Give me another hot dog and a cup of bilge water!"

"People versus Mathusek?" inquired Judge Watkins some hours later on the call of the calendar, looking quite vaguely as if he had never heard of the case before, round Part I, which was as usual crowded, hot, stuffy and smelling of unwashed linen and prisoners' lunch. "People versus Mathusek? What do you want done with this case, Mr. O'Brien?"

"Ready!" chanted the red-headed O'Brien, and, just as he had expected, the Hon. Raphael Hogan limbered up in his slow, genial way and said: "If Your Honor please, the defendant would like a few days longer to get his witnesses. Will Your Honor kindly adjourn the case for one week?"

He did not notice that the stenographer was taking down everything that he said.

"I observe," remarked Judge Watkins with apparent amiability, "that you have had five adjournments already. If The People's witnesses are here I am inclined to direct you to proceed. The defendant has been under indictment for six weeks. That ought to be long enough to prepare your defense."

"But, Your Honor," returned Hogan with pathos, "the witnesses are very hard to find. They are working people. I have spent whole evenings chasing after them. Moreover, the defendant is perfectly satisfied to have the case go over. He is anxious for an adjournment!"

"When did you last see him?"

"Yesterday afternoon."

The judge unfolded the papers and appeared to be reading them for the first time. He wasn't such a bad old actor himself, for he had already learned from Mr. Tutt that Hogan had not been near Tony for three weeks.

"Um—um! Did you represent the defendant in the police court?"

"Yes, Your Honor."

"Why did you waive examination?"

Hogan suddenly felt a lump swelling in his pharynx. What in hell was it all about?

"I—er—there was no use in fighting the case there. I hoped the grand jury would throw it out," he stammered.

"Did anybody ask you to waive examination?"

The swelling in Hogan's fat neck grew larger. Suppose McGurk or Delany were trying to put something over on him!

"No! Certainly not!" he replied unconvincingly. He didn't want to make the wrong answer if he could help it.

"You have an—associate, have you not? A Mr. Simpkins?"

"Yes, Your Honor." Hogan was pale now and little beads were gathering over his eyebrows.

"Where is he?"

"Downstairs in the magistrate's court."

"Officer," ordered the judge, "send for Mr. Simpkins. We will suspend until he can get here."

Then His Honor occupied himself with some papers, leaving Hogan standing alone at the bar trying to work out what it all meant. He began to wish he had never touched the damn case. Everybody in the courtroom seemed to be looking at him and whispering. He was most uncomfortable. Suppose that crooked cop had welshed on him! At the same instant in the back of the room a similar thought flashed through the mind of Delany. Suppose Hogan should welsh on him! Coincidentally both scoundrels turned sick at heart. Then came to each the simultaneous realization that neither could gain anything by giving the other away, and that the only thing possible for either was to stand pat. No, they must hang together or assuredly hang separately. Then the door opened and a tall officer entered, followed by a very nervous Mr. Joey Simpkins.

"Come up here!" directed the judge. "You are Mr. Hogan's assistant, are you not?"

"Yes, sir!" quavered the anxious Simpkins.

"How much money have you taken from Mrs. Mathusek?"

"Four hundred and thirty-five dollars."

"For what?" sharply.

"For protecting her son."

"Where? How?"

"Why—from his arrest to the present time—and for his defense here in General Sessions."

"Have either you or Mr. Hogan done anything as yet—except to waive examination in the police court?"

Mr. Simpkins turned hastily to Mr. Hogan, who realized that things were going badly.

"Your Honor," he interposed thickly, "this money was an agreed fee for my services as counsel. This examination seems to me somewhat uncalled for and unfair."

"Call Tony Mathusek to the bar!" suddenly ordered the judge.

It was a dangerous play, but Hogan decided to bluff it through.

"In view of the fact that I have not received my fee I shall refuse to appear for the defendant!" he announced brazenly.

"Indeed!" retorted the judge with sarcasm. "Then I will assign Mr. Ephraim Tutt to the defense. You two gentlemen will please sit down—but not leave the courtroom. We may need you."

At that moment, just as the defendant was led to the bar, Mr. Tutt emerged from behind the jury box and took his stand at Tony's side. Nothing much to look at before, the boy was less so now, with the prison pallor on his sunken little face. There was something about the thin neck, the half-open mouth and the gaunt, blinking, hollow eyes that suggested those of a helpless fledgling.

"Impanel a jury!" continued the judge, and Mr. Tutt conducted Tony inside the rail and sat down beside him at the table reserved for the defendant.

"It's all right, Tony!" he whispered. "The frame-up isn't on you this time, my lad."

Cowering in the back of the room Delany tried to hide himself among the spectators. Some devilish thing had gone wrong. He hadn't heard all that had passed between the judge and Hogan, but he had caught enough to perceive that the whole case had gone blooey.

Judge Watkins was wise! He was going after Hogan just as old Tutt would go after him, Delany. There was a singing in his head and the blood smarted in his eyes. He'd better beat it! Half bent over he started sneaking for the door.

"Who is that man trying to go out?" shouted the judge in terrifying tones that shook Delany to the ankles. Hastily he tried to sit down.

"Bring that man to the bar!"

Half blind with fear Delany attempted to make a show of bravado and swagger to the rail.

"What is your name?"

"Delany. Officer attached to the Second Precinct."

"What were you leaving the room for?"

Delany could not answer. His wits were befogged, his throat numb. He simply stared vacuously at Judge Watkins, his lips vibrating with fear.

"Sit down. No; take the stand!" cried Judge Watkins. "I'll try this case myself."

As if his foot were already attached to a ball and chain Delany dragged himself up—up—hundreds of feet up, it seemed—to the witness chair. As if from a mountain side he saw dim forms moving into the jury box, heard the judge and Mr. Tutt exchanging meaningless remarks. The faces before him grinned and gibbered at him like a horde of monkeys. They had got him at last—all for a few pieces of rotten beef! That lean, hungry wolfhound would tear his tongue out by the roots if he even opened his mouth; claw wide open his vitals. And old Tutt was fixing him with the eye of a basilisk and slowly turning him to stone. Somebody sure had welshed! He had once been in a side show at Coney Island where the room simulated the motion of an ocean steamer. The courtroom began to do the same—slanting this way and that and spinning obliquely round and round. Through the swirl of its gyrations he could see old Tutt's vulture eyes, growing bigger, fiercer, more sinister every instant. It was all up with him! It was an execution, and the crowd down below were thirsting for his blood, waiting to tear him to bits!

"You saw this boy throw a brick through Mr. Froelich's window, didn't you?" coaxed Judge Watkins insinuatingly. Delany sensed that the old white fox was trying to trick him—get him for perjury. No! He wouldn't perjure himself again! No! But what could he do? His head swung stupidly, swaying like a dazed bull's. The sweat poured from every pore in his vast bulk. A hoarse noise—like a death rattle—came from his throat. The room dissolved in waves of white and black. Then in a vertigo he toppled forward and pitched headlong to the floor.

Deacon Terry, star reporter for the *Tribune*, who happened to be there, told his city editor at noon that he had never passed such a pleasant morning. What he saw and heard really constituted, he alleged, a great big full front-page story "in a box"—though it got only four sticks on the eleventh page—being crowded out by the armistice. Why, he said, it was the damnedest thing ever! There had been no evidence against the defendant at all! And after the cop had collapsed Judge Watkins had refused to dismiss the case and directed Mr. Tutt to go on in his own way.

The proceeding had resolved itself into a criminal trial of Hogan and Simpkins. Tony's good character had been established in three minutes, and then half a dozen reputable witnesses had testified that the brick had been thrown by an entirely different boy. Finally, Sussman and his assistant both swore positively that Delany had been in the back of the tobacco shop with his back to the door, holding them up for cigars, when the crash came.

Terry wanted two columns; he almost cried when they cut his great big full-page story to:

SHYSTERS ACCUSED OF EXTORTION

A dramatic scene was enacted at the conclusion of a minor case in Part I of the General Sessions yesterday, when upon the motion of Ephraim Tutt, of the firm of Tutt & Tutt, Judge Simeon Watkins, sitting as a committing magistrate, held for the action of the grand jury Raphael B. Hogan and Joseph P. Simpkins, his assistant, for the crime of extortion, and directed that their case be referred to the Grievance Committee of the County Lawyers' Association for the necessary action for their disbarment.

Earlier in the trial a police officer named Delany, the supposed chief witness for the prosecution, fainted and fell from the witness chair. Upon his recovery he was then and there committed for perjury, in default of ten thousand dollars bail. It is understood that he has signified his willingness to turn state's evidence, but that his offer has not been accepted. So far as can be ascertained this is the first time either Hogan or Simpkins has been accused of a criminal offense. District

Attorney Peckham stated that in addition to separate indictments for extortion and perjury he would ask for another, charging all three defendants with the crime of conspiracy to obstruct the due administration of the law.

At the conclusion of the proceedings Judge Watkins permitted a voluntary collection to be taken up by Mr. Tutt on behalf of the accused among the jury, the court attendants and the spectators, which amounted to eleven hundred and eighty-nine dollars. In this connection the judge expressed the opinion that it was unfortunate that persons falsely accused of crime and unjustly imprisoned should have no financial redress other than by a special act of the legislature. The defendant in the case at bar had been locked up for six weeks. Among the contributions was found a new one-thousand-dollar bill.

"Talk about crime!" quoth the Deacon savagely to Charlie Still, of the *Sun*. "That feckless fool at the city desk committed assault, mayhem and murder on that story of mine!" Then he added pensively: "If I thought old man Tutt would slip me a thousand to soothe my injured feelings I'd go down and retain his firm myself!"

The Kid and the Camel

Breathes there the man with soul so dead
Who never to himself hath said,
This is my own, my native land!
—LAY OF THE LAST MINSTREL.

The shortest street in the world, Edgar Street, connects New York's financial center with the Levant. It is less than fifty feet through this tiny thoroughfare from the back doors of the great Broadway office buildings to Greenwich Street, where the letters on the window signs resemble contorted angleworms and where one is as likely to stumble into a man from Bagdad as from Boston. One can stand in the middle of it and with his westerly ear catch the argot of Gotham and with his easterly all the dialects of Damascus. And if through some unexpected convulsion of Nature 51 Broadway should topple over, Mr. Zimmerman, the stockbroker, whose office is on the sixth story, might easily fall clear of the Greek restaurant in the corner of Greenwich Street, roll twenty-five yards more down Morris Street, and find himself on Washington Street reading a copy of Al-Hoda and making his luncheon off *baha gannouge*, *majaddarah* and *milookeiah*, which, after all, are only eggplant salad, lentils and rice, and the popular favorite known as Egyptian Combination.

To most New Yorkers this is a section of the city totally unknown and unsuspected, yet existing as in a fourth dimension within a stone's throw—and nearer—of our busiest metropolitan artery—and there within one hundred yards of the aforesaid Mr. Zimmerman's office above the electric cars of Broadway, and within earshot of the hoots of many a multimillionaire's motor, on a certain evening something of an Oriental character was doing in the hallway of a house on Washington Street that subsequently played a part in the professional lives of Tutt & Tutt.

Out of the literally Egyptian darkness of the tenement owned by Abadallah Shanin Khaldi issued curious smothered sounds, together with an unmistakable, pungent, circuslike odor.

"Whack!"

There came an indignant grunt, followed by a flabby groan and a straining and squeaking of the jerry-built staircase as Kasheed Hassoun vigorously applied a lath to the horny backsides of Eset el Gazzar.

"Ascend, dog of a dog!" panted Kasheed. "Move thy accursed feet, O wizened hump! Daughter of Satan, give me room! Thou art squeezing out my life! Only go on, child of my heart! It is but a step upward, O Queen of the Nile. Hold the rope tight, Kalil!"

The camel obediently surged forward, breaking off a section of banister. Through the racket from the hallway above faintly came the voice of Kalil Majdalain.

"Her head is free of the ceiling. Quick, Kasheed! Turn her, thou, upon the landing!"

"Whack!" responded the lath in the hand of Kasheed Hassoun.

Step by step the gentle shaggy brute felt her way with feet, knees and nozzle up the narrow staircase. What was this but another of those bizarre experiences which any camel-of-the-world must expect in a land where the water wells squirted through a tube and men rode in chariots driven by fire?

"Whack!"

"Go on, darling of my soul!" whispered Kasheed. "Curses upon thy father and upon the mother that bore thee! Wilt thou not move?"

"Whack!"

"Ouch! She devil! Thou hast trod upon my foot!"

Outside, that the Western world might not suspect what was going on, Shaheen Mahfous and Shanin Saba unloaded with as much noise as possible a dray of paper for Meraat-ul-Gharb, the Daily Mirror. By and by a window on the fourth floor opened and the head of Kalil Majdalain appeared.

"*Mahabitcum!*" he grinned; which, being interpreted, means "Good fellowship to all!"

Then presently he and Kasheed joined the others upon the sidewalk, and, the rolls of paper having been delivered inside the pressroom, the four Syrians climbed upon the truck and drove to the restaurant of Ghabryel & Assad two blocks farther north, where they had a bit of *awamat*, coffee and cigarettes, and then played a game of cards, while in the attic of the tenement house Eset el Gazzar munched a mouthful of hay and tapped her interior reservoir for a drink of clear water, as she sighed through her valvelike nostrils and pouted with her cushioned lips, pondering upon the vagaries of quadrupedal existence.

Willie Toothaker, the office boy of Tutt & Tutt, had perfected a catapult along the lines of those used in the Siege of Carthage—form derived from the appendix of Allen and Greenough's Latin Grammar—which boded ill for the truck drivers of lower Gotham.

Since his translation from Pottsville Center, Willie's inventive genius had worked something of a transformation in the Tutt & Tutt offices, for he had devised several labor-saving expedients, such as a complicated series of pulleys for opening windows and automatically closing doors without getting up; which, since they actually worked, Mr. Tutt, being a pragmatist, silently, patiently and good-naturedly endured. To-day both partners were away in court and Willie had the office to himself with the exception of old Scraggs.

"Bet it'll shoot a block!" asserted Willie, replacing his gum, which he had removed temporarily to avert the danger of swallowing it in his excitement. "Caesar used one just like this—only bigger, of course. See that scuttle over on Washington Street? Bet I can hit it!"

"Bet you can't come within two hundred feet of it!" retorted the watery-eyed scrivener. "It's a lot further'n you think."

"'Tain't neither!" declared Willie. "I know how far it is! What can we shoot?"

Scraggs' eye wandered aimlessly round the room.

"Oh, I don't know."

"Got to be something with heft to it," said Willie. "'S got to overcome the resistance of the atmosphere."

"How about that paperweight?"

"'S too heavy."

"Well—"

"I know!" exclaimed William suddenly. "Gimme that little bottle of red ink. 'S just about right. And when it strikes it'll make a mark so's we can tell where we hit—like a regular target."

Scraggs hesitated.

"Ink costs money," he protested.

"But it's just the thing!" insisted Willie. "Besides, you can charge me for it in the cash account. Give it here!"

Conscience being thus satisfied the two eagerly placed the ink bottle in the proper receptacle, which Willie had fashioned out of a stogy box, twisted back the bow and aimed the apparatus at the slanting scuttle, which projected from a sort of penthouse upon the roof of the tenement house across the street.

"Now!" he exclaimed ecstatically. "Stand from under, Scraggs!"

He pressed a lever. There was a whang, a whistle—and the ink bottle hurtled in a beautiful parabola over Greenwich Street.

"Gee! look at her go!" cried Willie in triumph. "Straight's a string."

At exactly that instant—and just as the bottle was about to descend upon the penthouse—the scuttle opened and there was thrust forth a huge yellow face with enormous sooty lips wreathed in an unmistakable smile. On the long undulating neck the head resembled one of the grotesque manikins carried in circus parades. Eset el Gazzar in a search for air had discovered that the attic scuttle was slightly ajar.

"Gosh! A camel!" gasped Willie.

"Lord of love!" ejaculated Scraggs. "It sure is a camel!"

There was a faint crash and a tinkle of glass as the bottle of red ink struck the penthouse roof just over the beast's head and deluged it with its vermilion contents. Eset reared, shook her neck, gave a defiant grunt and swiftly withdrew her head into the attic.

Sophie Hassoun, the wife of Kasheed, seeing the violent change in Eset's complexion, wrung her hands.

"What hast thou done, O daughter of devils? Thou art bleeding! Thou hast cut thyself! Alack, mayhap thou wilt die, and then we shall be ruined! Improvident! Careless one! Cursed be thy folly! Hast thou no regard? And I dare not send for Doctor Koury, the veterinary, for then thy presence would be discovered and the gendarmes would come and take thee away. Would that we had left thee at Coney Island! O, great-granddaughter of Al Adha—sacred camel of the Prophet—why hast thou done this? Why hast thou brought misery upon us? *Awar! Awar!*"

She cast herself upon the improvised divan in the corner, while Eset, blinking, licked her big yellow hind hump, and tumbled forward upon her knees preparatory to sitting down herself.

"A camel!" repeated Willie, round-eyed. He counted the roofs dividing the penthouse from where Morris Street bisected the block. "Whoop!" he cried and dashed out of the office.

In less than four minutes Patrolman Dennis Patrick Murphy, who was standing on post on Washington Street in front of Nasheen Zereik's Embroidery Bazaar talking to Sardi Babu, saw a red-headed, pug-nosed urchin come flying round the corner.

"One—two—three—four—five. That's the house!" cried Willie Toothaker. "That's it!"

"What yer talkin' 'bout?" drawled Murphy.

"There's a camel in there!" shouted Willie, dancing up and down.

"Camel—yer aunt!" sneered the cop. "They couldn't get no camel in there!"

"There is! I seen it stick its head out of the roof!"

Sardi Babu, the oily-faced little dealer in pillow shams, smiled slyly. He had thick black ringlets, parted exactly down the middle of his scalp, hanging to his shoulders, and a luxuriant black curly beard reaching to his middle; in addition to which he wore a blue blouse and carpet slippers. He was a Maronite from Lebanon, and he and his had a feud with Hassoun, Majdalain, and all others who belonged to the sect headed by the Patriarch of Antioch.

"*Belki!*" he remarked significantly. "Perhaps his words are true! I have heard it whispered already by Lillie Nadowar, now the wife of Butros the confectioner. Moreover, I myself have seen hay on the stairs."

"Huh?" exclaimed Murphy. "We'll soon find out. Come along you, Babu! Show me where you was seein' the hay."

By this time those who had been lounging upon the adjacent doorstep had come running to see what was the matter, and a crowd had gathered.

"It is false—what he says!" declared Gadas Maloof the shoemaker. "I have sat opposite the house day and night for ten—fifteen years—and no camel has gone in. Camel! How could a camel be got up such narrow stairs?"

"But thou art a friend of Hassoun's!" retorted Fajala Mokarzel the grocer. "And," he added in a lower tone, "of Sophie Tadros, his wife."

There was a subdued snicker from the crowd, and Murphy inferred that they were laughing at him.

"But this man," he shouted wrathfully, pointing at Sardi Babu, "says you all know there's a camel up there. An' this kid's seen it! Come along now, both of you!"

There was an angry murmur from the crowd. Sardi Babu turned white.

"I said nothing!" he declared, trembling. "I made no complaint. The gendarme will corroborate me. What care I where Kasheed Hassoun stables his camel?"

Maloof shouldered his way up to him, and grasping the Maronite by the beard muttered in Arabic: "Thou dog! Go confess thy sins! For by the Holy Cross thou assuredly hast not long to live!"

Murphy seized Babu by the arm.

"Come on!" he ordered threateningly. "Make good now!" And he led him up the steps, the throng pressing close upon his heels.

"What's all this?" inquired Magistrate Burke bewilderedly an hour later as Officer Murphy entered the police court leading a tall Syrian in a heavy overcoat and green Fedora hat, and followed by several hundred black-haired, olive-skinned Levantines. "Don't let all those Dagos in here! Keep 'em out! This ain't a moving-picture palace!"

"Them ain't Dagos, judge," whispered Roony the clerk. "Them's Turks."

"They ain't neither Turks!" contradicted the stenographer, whose grammar was almost sublimated by comparison with Roony's. "They're Armenians—you can tell by their complexions."

"Well, I won't have 'em in here, whatever they are!" announced Burke. "I don't like 'em. What have you got, Murphy?"

"Shoo! Get out of here!" ordered the officer on duty.

The crowd, however, not understanding, only grinned.

"*Avanti! Alley! Mouch*! Beat it!" continued the officer, waving his arms and hustling those nearest toward the door.

The throng obediently fell back. They were a gentle, simple-minded lot, used in the old country to oppression, blackmail and tyranny, and burning with a religious fervor unknown to the pale heterodoxy of the Occident.

"This here," began Murphy, "is a complaint by Sardi Babu"—he swung the cowering little man with a twist before the bench—"against one Kasheed Hassoun for violating the health ordinances."

"No, no! I do not complain! I am not one who complains. It is nothing whatever to me if Kasheed Hassoun keeps a camel! I care not," cried Babu in Arabic.

"What's he talkin' about?" interrupted Burke. "I don't understand that sort of gibberish."

"He makes the complaint that this here Hassoun"—he indicated the tall man in the overcoat—"is violating Section 1093d of the regulations by keeping a camel in his attic."

"Camel!" ejaculated the magistrate. "In his attic!"

Murphy nodded.

"It's there all right, judge!" he remarked. "I've seen it."

"Is that straight?" demanded His Honor. "How'd he get it up there? I didn't suppose—"

Suddenly Sardi Babu threw himself fawning upon Hassoun.

"Oh, Kasheed Hassoun, I swear to thee that I made no complaint. It is a falsification of the gendarme! And there was a boy—a red and yellow boy—who said he had seen thy camel's head above the roofs! I am thy friend!"

He twisted his writhing snakelike fingers together. Hassoun regarded him coldly.

"Thou knowest the fate of informers and provocateurs—of spies—thou infamous Turk!" he answered through his teeth.

"A Turk! A Turk!" shrieked Sardi Babu frantically, beating the breast of his blue blouse. "Thou callest me a Turk! Me, the godson of Sarkis Babu and of Elias Stephan—whose fathers and grandfathers were Christians when thy family were worshipers of Mohammed. Blasphemy! Me, the godson of a bishop!"

"I also am godson of a bishop!" sneered Kasheed. "A properly anointed bishop! Without Tartar blood."

Sardi Babu grew purple.

"Ptha! I would spit upon the beard of such a bishop!" he shrieked, beside himself.

Hassoun slightly raised his eyebrows.

"Spit, then, infamous one—while thou art able!"

"Here, here!" growled Burke in disgust. "Keep 'em still, can't you? Now, what's all this about a camel?"

"That's the very scuttle, sir," asseverated Scraggs to the firm, as Tutt & Tutt, including Miss Wiggin, gazed down curiously out of their office windows at the penthouse upon the Washington Street roof which had been Willie's target of the day before. "I don't say," he continued by way of explanation, "that the camel stuck his head out because Willie hit the roof with the bottle—it was probably just a circumstance—but it looked that way. 'Bing!' went the ink bottle on the scuttle; and then—pop!—out came the camel like a jack-in-the-box."

"What became of the camel?" inquired Miss Wiggin, cherishing a faint hope that—pop!—it might suddenly appear again in the same way.

"The police took it away last night—lowered it out of the window with a block and tackle," answered the scrivener. "A sort of breeches buoy."

"I've heard of camel's-hair shawls but not of camel's-hair breeches!" murmured Tutt. "I suppose if a camel wore pants—well, my imagination refuses to contemplate the spectacle! Where's Willie?"

"He hasn't been in at all this morning!" said Miss Wiggin. "I'll warrant—"

"What?" demanded Mr. Tutt suspiciously.

"—he's somewhere with that camel," she concluded.

Now, Miss Minerva, as her name connoted, was a wise woman; and she had reached an unerring conclusion by two different and devious routes, to wit, intuition and logic, the same being the high road and low road of reason—high or low in either case as you may prefer. Thus logic: Camel—small boy.

Intuition: Small boy—camel. But there was here an additional element—a direct personal relationship between this particular small boy and this particular camel, rising out of the incident of the ink bottle. She realized that that camel must have acquired for William a peculiar quality—almost that of a possession—in view of the fact that he had put his mark upon it. She knew that Willie could no more stay away from the environs of that camel than said camel could remain in that attic. Indeed we might go on at some length expounding further this profound law of human nature that where there are camels there will be small boys; that, as it were, under such circumstances Nature abhors an infantile vacuum.

"If I know him, he is!" agreed Mr. Tutt, referring to William's probable proximity to Eset el Gazzar.

"Speaking of camels," said Tutt as he lit a cigarette, "makes me think of brass beds."

"Yes," nodded his partner. "Of course it would, naturally. What on earth do you mean?"

"I mean this," began Tutt, clearing his throat as if he were addressing twelve good and true men—"a camel is obviously an unusual—not to say peculiar—animal to be roosting over there in that attic. It is an exotic—if I may use that term. It is as exotic as a brass bed from Connecticut would be, or is, in Damascus or Lebanon. Now, therefore, a camel will as assuredly give cause for trouble in New York as a brass bed in Bagdad!"

"The right thing often makes trouble if put in the wrong place," pondered Mr. Tutt.

"Or the wrong thing in the right place!" assented Tutt. "Now all these unassimilated foreigners—"

"What have they got to do with brass beds in Lebanon?" challenged Miss Wiggin.

"Why," continued Tutt, "I am credibly informed that the American brass bed—particularly the double bed—owing to its importation into Asia Minor was the direct cause of the Armenian massacres."

"Tosh!" said Miss Wiggin.

"For a fact!" asserted Tutt. "It's this way—an ambassador told me so himself—the Turks, you know, are nuts on beds—and they think a great big brass family bed such as—you know—they're in all the department-store windows. Well, every Turk in every village throughout Asia Minor saves up his money to buy a brass bed—like a nigger buys a cathedral clock. Sign of superiority. You get me? And it becomes his most cherished household possession. If he meets a friend on the street he says to him naturally and easily, without too much conscious egotism, just as an American might say, 'By the way, have you seen my new limousine?'—he says to the other Turk, 'Oh, I say, old chap, do you happen to have noticed my new brass bed from Connecticut? They just put it off the steamer last week at Aleppo. Fatima's taking a nap in it now, but when she wakes up—'"

"What nonsense!" sniffed Miss Wiggin.

"It's not nonsense!" protested the junior partner. "Now listen to what happens. Some Armenian—the Armenians are the pawnbrokers of Asia Minor—moves into that village and in three months he has a mortgage on everything in it, including that brass bed. Then the Turkish Government, which regards him as an undesirable citizen, tells him to move along; and Mister Armenian piles all the stuff the inhabitants have mortgaged to him into an oxcart and starts on his way, escorted by the Sultan's troops. On top of the load is Yusuf Bulbul Ameer's brass bed. Yusuf looks out of his doorway and sees the bed moving off and rushes after it to protect his property.

"'Look here!' he shouts. 'Where are you going with my brass bed?'

"'It isn't yours!' retorts Mister Pawnbroker. 'It's mine. I loaned you eighty-seven piasters on it!'

"'But I've got an equity in it! You can't take it away!'

"'Of course I can!' replies the Armenian. 'Where I goeth it will go. The Turkish Government is responsible.'

"'Not much,' says Yusuf, grabbing hold of it, trying to pull it off the cart.

"'Hands off there!' yells the Armenian.

"Then there is a mix-up and everybody piles in—and there is a massacre!"

"That's a grand yarn!" remarked Mr. Tutt. "Still, it may be—"

"Bunk!" declared Miss Wiggin. "And what has that got to do with camels?"

"My point is," affirmed Tutt, waving his index finger—"my point is that just as a Yankee brass bed in Turkey will make certain trouble, so a Turkish camel in New York is bound to do the same thing."

A door slammed behind them and Willie's voice interrupted the conversation.

"Mr. Tutt! Mr. Tutt!" he cried hysterically. "There's been a murder down there—and we—I'm—partly responsible. I spent the night with the camel and he's—she's—all right—in Regan's Boarding Stable. But Kasheed is in the Tombs, and I told them you'd defend him. You will, won't you?"

Mr. Tutt looked at the excited boy.

"Who killed whom?" he asked correctly. "And where does the camel come in?"

"Somebody killed Sardi Babu," explained Willie. "I don't know exactly who did it—but they've arrested Kasheed Hassoun, the owner of Eset el Gazzar."

"Who?" roared Tutt.

"The camel. You see, nobody knew she was in the attic until I saw her stick her head out of the hole in the roof. Then I told Murphy and he went up and found her there. But Kasheed thought Sardi had told on him, you see, and nobody would believe him when he said he hadn't. The judge fined Kasheed twenty-five dollars, and he—Kasheed—accused Sardi of being a Turk and they had a big row right there in court. Nothing happened until the cops had got Eset out of the window and she was over at Regan's. I stayed there. Her head is bright red from the ink, you know. Then somebody went over to the restaurant where Sardi was and killed him. So you see, in a way, I'm to blame, and I didn't think you'd mind defending Kasheed, because he's a corker and if they electrocute him Eset will starve to death."

"I see," said. Mr. Tutt thoughtfully. "You think that by rights if anybody was going to get killed it ought to have been you?"

Willie nodded.

"Yes, sir," he assented.

And that is how a camel was the moving cause of the celebrated firm of Tutt & Tutt appearing as counsel in the case of The People against Kasheed Hassoun, charged with the crime of murder in the first degree for having taken the life of Sardi Babu with deliberation and premeditation and malice aforethought and against the peace of the People of the State of New York.

"And then there's this here Syrian murder case," groaned the chief clerk of the district attorney's office plaintively to his chief. "I don't know what to do with it. The defendant's been six months in the Tombs, with all the Syrian newspapers hollering like mad for a trial. He killed him all right, but you know what these foreign-language murder cases are, boss! They're lemons, every one of 'em!"

"What's the matter with it?" inquired the D.A. "It's a regular knock-down-and-drag-out case, isn't it? Killed him right in a restaurant, didn't he?"

"Sure! That part of it's all right," assented the chief clerk. "He killed him—yes! But how are you going to get an American jury to choose between witnesses who are quite capable of swearing that the corpse killed the defendant. How in hell can you tell what they're talking about, anyway?"

"You can't!" said the D.A. "Send the papers in to Pepperill and tell him on the side it'll make him famous. He'll believe you."

"But it'll take ten weeks to try it!" wailed the chief clerk.

"Well, send it down to old Wetherell, in Part Thirteen. He's got the sleeping sickness and it will be sort of soothing for him to listen to."

"Might wake him up?" suggested the other.

"You couldn't!" retorted the D.A. "What's the case about, anyhow?"

"It's about a camel," explained the subordinate hesitatingly.

The D.A. grinned. Said he: "It is easier for a camel to go through the eye of a needle than for a just prosecutor to convict a Syrian of murder. Well, old top, send for a couple of dozen Korans and hire rooms for the jury over Kaydoub, Salone & Dabut's and turn 'em loose on *kibbah arnabeiah, kashtah* and *halawee*."

Mr. William Montague Pepperill was a very intense young person, twenty-six years old, out of Boston by Harvard College. He had been born beneath the golden dome of the State House on Beacon Street, and from the windows of the Pepperill mansion his infant eyes had gazed smugly down upon the Mall and Frog Pond of the historic Common. There had been an aloof serenity about his life within the bulging front of the paternal residence with its ancient glass window panes—faintly tinged with blue, just as the blood in the Pepperill veins was also faintly tinged with the same color—his unimpeachable social position at Hoppy's and later on at Harvard—which he pronounced Haavaad—and the profound respect in which he was held at the law school in Cambridge, that gave Mr. W. Montague Pepperill a certain confidence in the impeccability of himself, his family, his relatives, his friends, his college, his habiliments and haberdashery, his deportment, and his opinions, political, religious and otherwise.

For W.M.P. the only real Americans lived on Beacon Hill, though a few perhaps might be found accidentally across Charles Street upon the made land of the Back Bay. A real American must necessarily also be a graduate of Harvard, a Unitarian, an allopath, belong to the Somerset Club and date back ancestrally at least to King Philip's War. W. Montague had, however, decided early in life that Boston was too small for him and that he owed a duty to the rest of the country.

So he had condescended to New York, where through his real American connections in law, finance and business he had landed a job in a political office where the aristocrats were all either Irish, Jews or Italians, who regarded him as an outlandish animal. It had been a strange experience for him. So had the discovery that graft, blackmail, corruption, vice and crime were not mere literary conventions, existing only for the theoretical purposes of novelists and playwrights, but were actualities frequently dealt with in metropolitan society. He had secured his appointment from a reform administration and he had been retained as a holdover by Peckham, the new district attorney, by reason of the fact that his uncle by marriage was a Wall Street banker who contributed liberally without prejudice to both political parties. This, however, W.M.P. did not know, and assumed that he was allowed to keep his four-thousand-dollar salary because the county could not get on without him. He was slender, wore a mouse-colored waistcoat, fawn tie and spats, and plastered his hair neatly down on each side of a glossy cranium that was an almost perfect sphere.

"Ah! Mr. William Montague Pepperill, I believe?" inquired Mr. Tutt with profound politeness from the doorway of W.M.P.'s cubicle, which looked into the gloomy light shaft of the Criminal Courts Building.

Mr. Pepperill finished what he was writing and then looked up.

"Yes," he replied. "What can I do for you?"

He did not ask Mr. Tutt his name or invite him to sit down.

The old lawyer smiled. He liked young men, even conceited young men; they were so enthusiastic, so confident, so uncompromising. Besides, W.M.P. was at heart, as Mr. Tutt perceived, a high-class sort of chap. So he smiled.

"My name is Tutt," said he. "I am counsel for a man named Hassoun, whom you are going to try for murder. You are, of course, perfectly familiar with the facts."

He fumbled in his waistcoat, produced two withered stogies and cast his eye along the wall.

"Would you—mind—if I sat down? And could I offer you a stogy?"

"Sit down—by all means," answered W.M.P. "No, thanks!"—to the stogy.

Mr. Tutt sat down, carefully placed his old chimney pot upside down on the window ledge, and stacked in it the bundle of papers he was carrying.

"I thought you might forgive me if I came to talk over the case a little with you. You see, there are so many things that a prosecutor has to consider—and which it is right that he should consider." He paused to light a match. "Now in this case, though in all probability my client is guilty there is practically no possibility of his being convicted of anything higher than manslaughter in the first degree. The defense will produce many witnesses—probably as many as the prosecution. Both sides will tell their stories in a language unintelligible to the jury, who must try to ascertain the true inwardness of the situation through an interpreter. They will realize that they are not getting the real truth—I mean the Syrian truth. As decent-minded men they won't dare to send a fellow to the chair whose defense they cannot hear and whose motives they do not either know or understand. They will feel, as I do and perhaps you do, that the only persons to do justice among Syrians are Syrians."

"Well," replied Mr. Pepperill politely, "what have you to propose?"

"That you recommend the acceptance of a plea of manslaughter in the second degree."

Deputy Assistant District Attorney William Montague Pepperill drew himself up haughtily. He regarded all criminal practitioners as semicrooks, ignorant, illiterate, rather dirty men—not in the real American class.

"I can do nothing of the kind," he answered sternly and very distinctly. "If these men seek the hospitality of our shores they must be prepared to be judged by our laws and by our standards of morality. I do not agree with you that our juridical processes are not adequate to that purpose. Moreover, I regard it as unethical—un-eth-i-cal—to accept a plea for a lesser degree of crime than that which the defendant has presumptively committed."

Mr. Tutt regarded him with undisguised admiration.

"Your sentiments do you honor, Mr. Pepperill!" he returned. "You are sure you do not mind my smoke? But of course my client is presumed innocent. I am very hopeful—almost confident—of getting him off entirely. But rather than take the very slight chance of a conviction for murder I am letting discretion take the place of valor and offer to have him admit his guilt of manslaughter."

"I guess," answered Pepperill laconically, indulging in his only frequent solecism, "that you wouldn't offer to plead to manslaughter unless you felt pretty sure your client was going to the chair! Now—"

Mr. Tutt suddenly rose.

"My young friend," he interrupted, "when Ephraim Tutt says a thing man to man—as I have been speaking to you—he means what he says. I have told you that I expected to acquit my client. My only reason for offering a plea is the very slight—and it is a very slight—chance that an Arabian quarrel can be made the basis of a conviction for murder. When you know me better you will not feel so free to impugn my sincerity. Are you prepared to entertain my suggestion or not?"

"Most certainly not!" retorted W.M.P. with the shadow of a sneer.

"Then I will bid you good-day," said Mr. Tutt, taking his hat from the window ledge and turning to the door. "And—you young whippersnapper," he added when once it had closed behind him and he had turned to shake his lean old fist at the place where W.M.P. presumably was still sitting, "I'll show you how to treat a reputable member of the bar old enough to be your grandfather! I'll take the starch out of your darned Puritan collar! I'll harry you and fluster you and heckle you and make a fool of you, and I'll roll you up in a ball and blow you out the window, and turn old Hassoun loose for an Egyptian holiday that will make old Rome look like thirty piasters! You pinheaded, pretentious, pompous, egotistical, niminy-piminy—"

"Well, well, Mr. Tutt, what's the matter?" inquired Peckham, laying his hand on the old lawyer's shoulder. "What's Peppy been doing to you?"

"It isn't what he's been doing to me; it's what I'm going to do to him!" returned Mr. Tutt grimly. "Just wait and see!"

"Go to it!" laughed the D.A. "Eat him alive! We're throwing him to the lions!"

"No decent lion would want him!" retorted Mr. Tutt. "He might maul him a little, but I won't. I'm just going to give him a full opportunity to test his little proposition that the institutions of these jolly old United States are perfectly adapted to settle quarrels among all the polyglot prevaricators of the world and administer justice among people who are still in a barbarous or at least in a patriarchal state. He's young, and he don't understand that a New York merchant is entirely too conscientious to find a man guilty on testimony that he would discount heavily in his own business."

"Go as far as you like," laughed Peckham.

"Oh, I'm only going as far as Bagdad," answered Mr. Tutt.

Deputy Assistant District Attorney Pepperill complacently set about the preparation of his case, utterly unconscious of the dangers with which his legal path was beset. As he sat at his shiny oaken desk and pressed the button that summoned the stenographer it seemed to him the simplest thing in the world to satisfy any jury of what had taken place and the summit of impudent audacity on the part of Mr. Tutt to have suggested that Hassoun should be dealt with otherwise than a first-degree murderer. And it should be added parenthetically that W.M.P., in spite of his New England temperament, had a burning ambition to send somebody to the electric chair.

In truth, on its face the story as related by Fajala Mokarzel and the other friends of Sardi Babu the deceased pillow-sham vender was simplicity itself. Besides Sardi Babu and Mokarzel there had been Nicola Abbu, the confectioner; Menheem Shikrie, the ice-cream vendor; Habu Kahoots, the showman; and David Elias, a pedler. All six of them, as they claimed, had been sitting peacefully in Ghabryel & Assad's restaurant, eating *kibbah arnabeiah* and *mamoul*. Sardi had ordered *sheesh kabab*. It was about nine o'clock in the evening, and they were talking politics and drinking coffee and smoking cigarettes.

Suddenly Kasheed Hassoun, accompanied by a smaller and much darker man, had entered and striding up to the table exclaimed in a threatening manner: "Where is he who did say that he would spit upon the beard of my bishop?"

Thereupon Sardi Babu had risen and answered: "Behold, I am he."

Immediately Kasheed Hassoun, and while his accomplice held them at bay with a revolver, had leaned across the table and grabbing Sardi by the throat had broken his neck. Then the smaller man had fired off his pistol and both of them had run away. The simplest story ever told. There was everything the law required to send any murderer to the chair, and little Mr. Pepperill had a diagram made of the inside of the restaurant and a photograph of the outside of it, and stamped the indictment in purple ink: Ready for Trial.

Contemporaneously Mr. Tutt was giving his final instructions to Mr. Bonnie Doon, his stage manager, director of rehearsals and general superintendent of arrangements in all cases requiring an extra-artistic touch.

"It's too bad we can't cart a few hundred cubic feet of the Sahara into the court room and divert the Nile down Center Street, but I guess you can produce sufficient atmosphere," he said.

"I could all right—if I had a camel," remarked Bonnie.

"Atmosphere is necessary," continued Mr. Tutt. "Real atmosphere! Have 'em in native costume—beads, red slippers, hookahs, hoochi-koochis."

"I get you," replied Mr. Doon. "You want a regular Turkish village. Well, we'll have it all right. I'll engage the entire Streets of Cairo production from Coney and have Franklin Street crowded with goats, asses and dromedaries. I might even have a caravan pitch its tents alongside the Tombs."

"You can't lay it on too strong," declared Mr. Tutt. "But you don't need to go off Washington Street. And, Bonnie, remember—I want every blessed Turk, Greek, Armenian, Jew, Arab, Egyptian and Syrian that saw Sardi Babu kill Kasheed Hassoun."

"You mean who saw Kasheed Hassoun kill Sardi Babu," corrected Bonnie.

"Well—whichever way it was," agreed Mr. Tutt.

When at length the great day of the trial arrived Judge Wetherell, ascending the bench in Part Thirteen, was immediately conscious of a subtle Oriental smell that emanated from no one could say where, but which none the less permeated the entire court room. It seemed to be a curious compound of incense, cabbage, garlic and eau de cologne, with a suggestion of camel. The room was entirely filled with Syrians. One row of benches was occupied by a solemn group of white-bearded patriarchs who looked as if they had momentarily paused on a pilgrimage to Mecca. All over the room rose the murmur of purring Arabic. The stenographer was examining a copy of Meraat-ul-Gharb, the clerk a copy of El Zeman, and in front of the judge's chair had been laid a copy of Al-Hoda.

His honor gave a single sniff, cast his eye over the picturesque throng, and said: "Pst! Captain! Open that window!" Then he picked up the calendar and read: "'People versus Kasheed Hassoun—Murder.'"

The stenographer was humming to himself:
Bagdad is a town in Turkey
On a camel tall and jerky.

"Are both sides ready to try this case?" inquired Judge Wetherell, choking a yawn. He was a very stout judge and he could not help yawning.

Deputy Assistant District Attorney Pepperill and Mr. Tutt rose in unison, declaring that they were. At or about this same moment the small door in the rear of the room opened and an officer appeared, leading in Kasheed Hassoun. He was an imposing man, over six feet in height, of dignified carriage, serious mien, and finely chiseled features. Though he was dressed as a European there was nevertheless something indefinably suggestive of the East in the cut of his clothes; he wore no waistcoat and round his waist was wound a strip of crimson cloth. His black eyes glinted through lowering brows, wildly, almost fiercely, and he strode haughtily beside his guard like some unbroken stallion of the desert.

"Well, you may as well proceed to select a jury," directed the court, putting on his glasses and studying his copy of Al-Hoda with interest. Presently he beckoned to Pepperill.

"Have you seen this?" he asked.

"No, Your Honor. What is it?"

"It's a newspaper published by these people," explained His Honor. "Rather amusing, isn't it?"

"I didn't know they had any special newspaper of their own," admitted Pepperill.

"They've got eight right in New York," interjected the stenographer.

"I notice that this paper is largely composed of advertisements," commented Wetherell. "But the advertisers are apparently scattered all over the world—Chicago; Pittsburgh; Canton; Winnipeg; Albuquerque; Brooklyn; Tripoli; Greenville, Texas; Pueblo; Lawrence, Massachusetts; Providence, Rhode Island; Fall River; Detroit—"

"Here's one from Roxbury, Massachusetts, and another from Mexico City," remarked the clerk delightedly.

"And here's one from Paris, France," added the stenographer. "Say! Some travelers!"

"Well, go on getting the jury," said the judge, yawning again and handing the paper to the clerk.

At that moment Mr. Salim Zahoul, the interpreter procured by Mr. Pepperill, approached, bowed and, twisting his purple mustache, addressed the court: "Your Excellence: I haf to zay dat dees papaire eet haf articles on zis affair—ze *memkaha*—zat are not diplomatique."

Judge Wetherell blinked at him.

"Who's this man?" he demanded.

"That's the interpreter," explained W.M.P.

"Interpreter!" answered the court. "I can't understand a word he says!"

"He was the best I could get," apologized Pepperill, while the countenance of Mr. Zahoul blazed with wrath and humiliation. "It's very difficult to get a fluent interpreter in Arabic."

"Well, just interpret what *he* says to *me*, will you?" kindly requested His Honor.

"I zay," suddenly exploded Zahoul—"dees papaire eet half contemptuous article on ze *menkaha* zat dees Kasheed Hassoun not kill dees Sardi Babu!"

"He says," translated Pepperill, "that the newspaper contains an indiscreet article in favor of the defense. I had no idea there would be any improper attempt to influence the jury."

"What difference does it make, anyway?" inquired His Honor. "You don't expect any juryman is going to read that thing, do you? Why, it looks as if a bumblebee had fallen into an ink bottle and then had a fit all over the front page."

"I don't suppose—" began Pepperill.

"Go on and get your jury!" admonished the court.

So the lion and the lamb in the shape of Mr. Tutt and Pepperill proceeded to select twelve gentlemen to pass upon the issue who had never been nearer to Syria than the Boardwalk at Atlantic City and who only with the utmost attention could make head or tail of what Mr. Salim Zahoul averred that the witnesses were trying to say. Moreover, most of the talesmen evinced a profound distrust of their own ability to do justice between the People and the defendant and a curious desire to be relieved from service. However, at last the dozen had been chosen and sworn, the congestion of the court room slightly relieved, Mr. Zahoul somewhat appeased, and Mr. William Montague Pepperill rose to outline his very simple case to the jury.

There was, he explained, no more difficulty in administering justice in the case of a foreigner than of anyone else. All were equal in the eyes of the law—equally presumed to be innocent, equally responsible when proved guilty. And he would prove Kasheed Hassoun absolutely guilty—guilty beyond a reasonable doubt, beyond any doubt. He would produce five—five reputable witnesses who would swear that Hassoun had murdered Sardi Babu; and he prophesied that he would unhesitatingly demand at the end of the trial such an unequivocal, fearless, honest expression of their collective opinion as would permanently fix Mr. Kasheed Hassoun so that he could do no more harm. He expressed it more elegantly but that was the gist of it. He himself was as sincere and honest in his belief in his ability to establish the truth of his claim as he was in the justice of his cause. Alas, he was far too young to realize that there is a vast difference between knowing the truth and being able to demonstrate what it is!

In proper order he called the photographer who had taken the picture of the restaurant, the draftsman who had made the diagram of the interior, the policeman who had arrested Hassoun, the doctor who had performed the official autopsy upon the unfortunate Babu, and the five Syrians who had been present when the crime was perpetrated. Each swore by all that was holy that Kasheed Hassoun had done exactly as outlined by Assistant District Attorney Pepperill—and swore it word for word, *verbatim et literatim, in iisdem verbis, sic,* and yet again exactly. Their testimony mortised and tenoned in a way to rejoice a cabinet-maker's heart. And at first to the surprise and later to the dismay of Mr. Pepperill, old man Tutt asked not one of them a single question about the murder. Instead he merely inquired in a casual way where they came from, how they got there, what they did for a living, and whether they had ever made any contradictory statement as to what had occurred, and as his cross-examination of Mr. Habu Kahoots was typical of all the rest it may perhaps be set forth as an example, particularly as Mr. Kahoots spoke English, which the others did not.

"And den," asserted Mr. Kahoots stolidly, "Kasheed Hassoun, he grab heem by ze troat and break hees neck."

He was a short, barrel-shaped man with curly ringlets, fat, bulging cheeks, heavy double chin and enormous paunch, and he wore a green worsted waistcoat and his fingers were laden with golden rings.

"Ah!" said Mr. Tutt complaisantly. "You saw all that exactly as you have described it?"

"Yes, sair!"
"Where were you born?"
"Acre, Syria."
"How long have you been in the United States?"
"Tirty years."
"Where do you live?"
"Augusta, Georgia."
"What's your business?"

Mr. Kahoots visibly expanded.

"I have street fair and carnival of my own. I have electric theater, old plantation, Oriental show, snake exhibit and merry-go-round."

"Well, well!" exclaimed Mr. Tutt. "You are certainly a capitalist! I hope you are not financially overextended!"

Mr. Pepperill looked pained, not knowing just how to prevent such jocoseness on the part of his adversary.

"I object," he muttered feebly.

"Quite properly!" agreed Mr. Tutt. "Now, Mr. Kahoots, are you a citizen of the United States?"

Mr. Kahoots looked aggrieved.

"Me? No! Me no citizen. I go back sometime Acre and build moving-picture garden and ice-cream palace."

"I thought so," commented Mr. Tutt. "Now what, pray, were you doing in the Washington Street restaurant?"

"Eating *kibbah arnabeiah* and *mamoul*."

"I mean if you live in Augusta how did you happen to be in New York at precisely that time?"

"Eh?"

"How you come in New York?" translated Mr. Tutt, while the jury laughed.

"Just come."

"But why?"

"Just come."

"Yes, yes; but you didn't come on just to be present at the murder, did you?"

Kahoots grinned.

"I just come to walk up and down."

"Where—walk up and down?"

"On Washington Street. I spend the winter. I do nothing. I rich man."

"How long did you stay when you just came on?"

"Tree days. Then I go back."

"Why did you go back?"

"I dunno. Just go back."

Mr. Tutt sighed. The jury gave signs of impatience.

"Look here!" he demanded. "How many times have you gone over your story with the district attorney?"

"Nevvair."

"What?"

"I nevvair see heem."

"Never see whom?"
"Dees man—judge."
"I'm not talking about the judge."
"I nevvair see no one."
"Didn't you tell the Grand Jury that Hassoun stabbed Babu with a long knife?"
"I dunno heem!"
"Who?"
"Gran' Jury."
"Didn't you go into a big room and put your hand on a book and swear?"
"I no swear—ever!"
"And tell what you saw?"
"I tell what I saw."
"What did you see?"
"I saw Hassoun break heem hees neck."
"Didn't you say first that Hassoun stabbed Babu?"
"No—nevvair!"
"Then didn't you come back and say he shot him?"
"No—nevvair!"
"And finally, didn't you say he strangled him—after you had heard that the coroner's physician had decided that that was how he was killed?"
"Yes—he break heem hees neck."

Mr. Kahoots was apparently very much bored, but he was not bored in quite the same way as the judge, who, suddenly rousing himself, asked Mr. Tutt if he had any basis for asking such questions.

"Why, certainly," answered the old lawyer quietly. "I shall prove that this witness made three absolutely contradictory statements before the Grand Jury."

"Is that so, Mister District Attorney?"

"I don't know," replied Pepperill faintly. "I had nothing to do with the proceedings before the Grand Jury."

Judge Wetherell frowned.

"It would seem to me," he began, "as if a proper preparation of the case would have involved some slight attention to—Well, never mind! Proceed, Mr. Tutt."

"Kahoots!" cried the lawyer sternly. "Isn't it a fact that you have been convicted of crime yourself?"

The proprietor of the merry-go-round drew himself up indignantly.

"Me? No!"

"Weren't you convicted of assault on a man named Rafoul Rabyaz?"

"Me? Look here, sir! I tell you 'bout dat! This Rafoul Rabyaz he my partner, see, in pool, billiard and cigar business on Greenwich Street. This long time ago. Years ago. We split up. I sell heem my shares, see. I open next door—pool table, café and all. But I not get full half the stock. I not get the tablecloth, see. I was of the tablecloth you know short. It don't be there. I go back there that time. I see heem. I say, 'We don't count those tablecloth.' He say, 'Yes.' I say,'No.' He say,'Yes.' I say 'No.' He say, 'Yes.' I say, 'No'—"

"For heaven's sake," exclaimed Judge Wetherell, "don't say that again!"

"Yes, sair," agreed the showman. "All right. I say, 'No.' I say, 'You look in the book.' He say, 'No.' We each take hold of the cloth. I have a knife. I cut cloth in two. I give heem half. I take half. I say, 'You take half; I take half.' He say, 'Go to hell!'"

He waved his hand definitively.

"Well?" inquired Mr. Tutt anxiously.

"Dat's all!" answered Mr. Kahoots.

One of the jurymen suddenly coughed and thrust his handkerchief into his mouth.

"Then you stuck your knife into him, didn't you?" suggested Mr. Tutt.

"Me? No!"

Mr. Tutt shrugged his shoulders and pursed his lips.

"You were convicted, weren't you?"

"I call twenty witness!" announced Mr. Kahoots with a grand air.

"You don't need to!" retorted Mr. Tutt. "Now tell us why you had to leave Syria?"

"I go in camel business at Coney Island," answered the witness demurely.

"What!" shouted the lawyer. "Didn't you run away from home because you were convicted of the murder of Fatima, the daughter of Abbas?"

"Me? No!" Mr. Kahoots looked shocked.

Mr. Tutt bent over and spoke to Bonnie Doon, who produced from a leather bag a formidable document on parchment-like paper covered with inscriptions in Arabic and adorned with seals and ribbons.

"I have here, Your Honor," said he, "the record of this man's conviction in the Criminal Court in Beirut, properly exemplified by our consuls and the embassy at Constantinople. I have had it translated, but if Mr. Pepperill prefers to have the interpreter read it—"

"Show it to the district attorney!" directed His Honor.

Pepperill looked at it helplessly.

"You may read your own translation," said the court drowsily.

Mr. Tutt bowed, took up the paper and faced the jury.

"This is the official record," he announced. "I will read it.

"'In the name of God.

"'On a charge of the murder of the gendarmes Nejib Telhoon and Abdurrahman and Ibrahim Aisha and Fatima, daughter of Hason Abbas, of the attack on certain nomads, of having fired on them with the intent of murder, of participation and assistance in the act of murder, of having shot on the regular troops, of assisting in the escape of some offenders and of having drawn arms on the regular troops, during an uprising on Sunday, January 24, 1303—Mohammedan style—between the inhabitants of the Mezreatil-Arab quarter in Beirut and the nomads who had pitched their tents near by, the following arrested persons, namely—Metri son of Habib Eljemal and Habib son of Mikael Nakash and Hanna son of Abdallah Elbaitar and Elias Esad Shihada and Tanous son of Jerji Khedr and Habib son of Aboud Shab and Elias son of Metri Nasir and Khalil son of Mansour Maoud and Nakhle son of Elias Elhaj and Nakhle son of Berkat Minari and Antoon son of Berkat Minari and Lutfallah son of

Jerji-Kefouri and Jabran Habib Bishara and Kholil son of Lutf Dahir and Nakhle Yousif Eldefoumi, all residents of the said quarter and Turkish subjects, and their companions, sixty-five fugitives, namely—Isbir Bedoon son of Abdallah Zerik and Elias son of Kanan Zerik and Amin Matar and Jerji Ferhan alias Baldelibas and Habu son of Hanna Kahoots and—'"

Deputy Assistant District Attorney Pepperill started doubtfully to his feet.

"If the court please," he murmured in a sickly voice, "I object. In the first place I don't know anything about this record—and I object to it on that ground; and in the second place a trial and conviction in the absence of a defendant under our law is no conviction at all."

"But this man is a Turkish subject and it's a good conviction in Turkey," argued Mr. Tutt.

"Well, it isn't here!" protested Pepperill.

"You're a little late, aren't you?" inquired His Honor. "It has all been read to the jury. However, I'll entertain a motion to strike out—"

"I should like to be heard on the question," said Mr. Tutt quickly. "This is an important matter."

Unexpectedly a disgruntled-looking talesman in the back row held up his hand.

"I'd like to ask a question myself," he announced defiantly, almost arrogantly, after the manner of one with a grievance. "I'm a hard-working business man. I've been dragged here against my will to serve on this jury and decide if this defendant murdered somebody or other. I don't see what difference it makes whether or not this witness cut a tablecloth in two or murdered Fatima, the daughter of What's his Name. I want to go home—sometime. If it is in order I'd like to suggest that we get along."

Judge Wetherell started and peered with a puzzled air at this bold shatterer of established procedure.

"Mister Juryman," said he severely, "these matters relate directly to the credibility of the witness. They are quite proper. I—I—am—surprised—"

"But, Your Honor," expostulated the iconoclast upon the back row, "I guess nobody is going to waste much time over this Turkish snake charmer! Ain't there a policeman or somebody we can believe who saw what happened?"

"Bang!" went the judicial gavel.

"The juryman will please be silent!" shouted Judge Wetherell. "This is entirely out of order!" Then he quickly covered his face with his handkerchief. "Proceed!" he directed in a muffled tone.

"Where were we?" asked Mr. Tutt dreamily.

"Fatima, the daughter of Abbas," assisted the foreman, sotto voce.

"And I objected to Fatima, the daughter of Abbas!" snapped Pepperill.

"Well, well!" conceded Mr. Tutt. "She's dead, poor thing! Let her be. That is all, Mr. Kahoots."

It is difficult to describe the intense excitement these digressions from the direct testimony occasioned among the audience. The reference to the billiard-table cover and the murder of the unfortunate Fatima apparently roused long-smoldering fires. A group of Syrians by the window broke into an unexpected altercation, which had to be quelled by a court officer, and when quiet was restored the jury seemed but slightly attentive to the precisely similar yarns of Nicola Abbu, Menheem Shikrie, Fajal Mokarzel and David Elias, especially as the minutes of the Grand Jury showed that they had sworn to three entirely different sets of facts regarding the cause of Babu's death. Yet when the People rested it remained true that five witnesses, whatever the jury may have thought of them, had testified that Hassoun strangled Sardi Babu. The jury turned expectantly to Mr. Tutt to hear what he had to say.

"Gentlemen," he said quietly, "the defense is very simple. None of the witnesses who have appeared here was in fact present at the scene of the homicide at all. I shall call some ten or twelve reputable Syrian citizens who will prove to you that Kasheed Hassoun, my client, with a large party of friends was sitting quietly in the restaurant when Sardi Babu came in with a revolver in his hand, which he fired at Hassoun, and that then, and only then, a small dark man whose identity cannot be established—evidently a stranger—seized Babu before he could fire again, and killed him—in self-defense."

Mr. William Montague Pepperill's jaw dropped as if he had seen the ghost of one of his colonial ancestors. He could not believe that he had heard Mr. Tutt correctly. Why, the old lawyer had the thing completely turned round! Sardi Babu hadn't gone to the restaurant. He had been in the restaurant, and it had been Kasheed Hassoun who had gone there.

Yet, one by one, placidly, imperturbably, the dozen witnesses foretold by Mr. Tutt, and gathered in by Bonnie Doon, marched to the chair and swore upon the Holy Bible that it was even as Mr. Tutt had said, and that no such persons as Mokarzel, Kahoots, Abbu, Shikrie and Elias had been in the restaurant at any time that evening, but on the contrary that they, the friends of Hassoun, had been there eating Turkish pie—a few might have had mashed beans with *taheenak*—when Sardi Babu, apparently with suicidal intent, entered alone to take vengeance upon the camel owner.

"That is all. That is our case," said Mr. Tutt as the last Syrian left the stand.

But there was no response from the bench. Judge Wetherell had been dozing peacefully for several hours. Even Pepperill could not avoid a decorous smile. Then the clerk pulled out the copy of Al-Hoda and rustled it, and His Honor, who had been dreaming that he was riding through the narrow streets of Bagdad upon a jerky white dromedary so tall that he could peek through the latticed balconies at the plump, black-eyed odalisques within the harems, slowly came back from Turkey to New York.

"Gentlemen of the jury," said he, pulling himself together, "the defendant here is charged by the Grand Jury with having murdered Fatima the daughter of Abbas—I beg your pardon! I mean—who was it?—one Sardi Babu. I will first define to you the degrees of homicide—"

One day three months later, after Kasheed Hassoun had been twice tried upon the same testimony and the jury had disagreed—six to six, each time—Mr. Tutt, who had overstayed his lunch hour at the office, put on his stovepipe hat and strolled along Washington Street, looking for a place to pick up a bite to eat. It was in the middle of the afternoon and most of the stores were empty, which was all the more to his liking. He had always wanted to try some of that Turkish pie that they had all talked so much about at the trial. Presently a familiar juxtaposition of names caught his eye—Ghabryel & Assad. The very restaurant which had been the scene of the crime! Curiously, he turned in there. Like all the other places it was deserted, but at the sound of his footsteps a little Syrian boy not more than ten years old came from behind the screen at the end of the room and stood bashfully awaiting his order.

Mr. Tutt smiled one of his genial weather-beaten smiles at the youngster and glancing idly over the bill of fare ordered *biklama* and coffee. Then he lit a stogy and stretched his long legs comfortably out under the narrow table. Yes, this was the very spot where either Sardi Babu and his friends had been sitting the night of the murder or Kasheed Hassoun and his friends—one or the other; he wondered if anybody would ever know which. Was it possible that in this humdrum little place human passions had been roused to the taking of life on account of some mere difference in religious dogma? Was this New York? Was it possible to Americanize these people? A door clattered in the rear, and from behind the screen again emerged the boy carrying a tray of pastry and coffee.

"Well, my little man," said Mr. Tutt, "do you work here?"

"Oh, yes," answered the embryonic citizen. "My father, he owns half the store. I go to school every day, but I work here afterward. I got a prize last week."

"What sort of a prize?"

"I got the English prize."

The lawyer took the child's hand and pulled him over between his knees. He was an attractive lad, clean, responsive, frank, and his eyes looked straight into Mr. Tutt's.

"Sonny," he inquired his new friend, "are you an American?"

"Me? Sure! You bet I'm an American! The old folks—no! You couldn't change 'em in fifty years. They're just what they always were. They don't want anything different. They think they're in Syria yet. But me—say, what do you think? Of course I'm an American!"

"That's right!" answered Mr. Tutt, offering him a piece of pastry. "And what is your name?"

"George Nasheen Assad," answered the boy, showing a set of white teeth.

"Well, George," continued the attorney, "what has become of Kasheed Hassoun?"

"Oh, he's down at Coney Island. He runs a caravan. He has six camels. I go there sometimes and he lets me ride for nothing. I know who you are," said the little Syrian confidently, as he took the cake. "You're the great lawyer who defended Kasheed Hassoun."

"That's right. How did you know that, now?"

"I was to the trial."

"Do you think he ought to have been let off?" asked Mr. Tutt whimsically.

"I don't know," returned the child. "I guess you did right not to call me as a witness."

Mr. Tutt wrinkled his brows.

"Eh? What? You weren't a witness, were you?"

"Of course I was!" laughed George. "I was here behind the screen. I saw the whole thing. I saw Kasheed Hassoun come in and speak to Sardi Babu, and I saw Sardi draw his revolver, and I saw Kasheed tear it out of his hand and strangle him."

Mr. Tutt turned cold.

"You saw that?" he challenged.

"Sure."

"How many other people were there in the restaurant?" inquired Mr. Tutt.

"Nobody at all," answered George in a matter-of-fact tone. "Only Kasheed and Sardi. Nobody else was in the restaurant."

Contempt of Court

The court can't determine what is honor.—Chief Baron Bowes, 1743.

I know what my code of honor is, my lord, and I intend to adhere to it.—John O'Conner, M.P., in Parnell Commission's Proceedings, 103d Day; Times Rep. pt. 28, pp. 19 *ff.*

Well, honor is the subject of my story.—Julius Caesar, Act I, Sc 2.

"What has become of Katie—the second waitress?" asked Miss Althea Beekman of Dawkins, her housekeeper, as she sat at her satinwood desk after breakfast. "I didn't see her either last night or this morning."

Dawkins, who was a mid-Victorian, flushed awkwardly.

"I really had to let the girl go, ma'am!" she explained with an outraged air. "I hardly know how to tell you—such a thing in this house! I couldn't possibly have her round. I was afraid she might corrupt the other girls, ma'am—and they are such a self-respecting lot—almost quite ladylike, ma'am. So I simply paid her and told her to take herself off."

Miss Beekman looked pained.

"You shouldn't have turned her out into the street like that, Dawkins!" she expostulated. "Where has she gone?"

Dawkins gazed at her large feet in embarrassment.

"I don't know, ma'am," she admitted. "I didn't suppose you'd want her here so I sent her away. It was quite inconvenient, too—with the servant problem what it is. But I'm hoping to get another this afternoon from Miss Healey's."

Miss Beekman was genuinely annoyed.

"I am seriously displeased with you, Dawkins!" she returned severely. "Of course, I am shocked at any girl in my household misbehaving herself, but—I—wouldn't want her to be sent away—under such circumstances. It would be quite heartless. Yes, I am very much disturbed!"

"I'm sorry, ma'am," answered the housekeeper penitently. "But I was only thinking of the other girls."

"Well, it's too late to do anything about it now," repeated her mistress. "But I'm sorry, Dawkins; very sorry, indeed. We have responsibilities toward these people! However—this is Thursday, isn't it?—we'll have veal for lunch as usual—and she was so pretty!" she added inconsequently.

"H'm. That was the trouble!" sniffed the housekeeper. "We're well rid of her. You'd think a girl would have some consideration for her employer—if nothing else. In a sense she is a guest in the house and should behave herself as such!"

"Yes, that is quite true!" agreed her employer. "Still—yes, Brown Betty is very well for dessert. That will do, Dawkins."

Behind the curtain of this casual conversation had been enacted a melodrama as intensely vital and elemental as any of Shakespeare's tragedies, for the day Dawkins had fired Katie O'Connell—"for reasons," as she said—and told her to go back where she came from or anywhere she liked for that matter, so long as she got out of her sight, Katie's brother Shane in the back room of McManus' gin palace gave Red McGurk—for the same "reasons"—a certain option and, the latter having scornfully declined to avail himself of it, had then and there put a bullet through his neck. But this, naturally, Miss Beekman did not know.

As may have been already surmised Miss Althea was a gracious, gentle and tender-hearted lady who never knowingly would have done a wrong to anybody and who did not believe that simply because God had been pleased to call her into a state of life at least three stories higher than her kitchen she was thereby relieved from her duty toward those who occupied it. Nevertheless, from the altitude of those three stories she viewed them as essentially different from herself, for she came of what is known as "a long line of ancestors." As, however, Katie O'Connell and Althea Beekman were practically contemporaries, it is somewhat difficult to understand how one of them could have had a succession of ancestors that was any longer than that of the other. Indeed, Miss Beekman's friend, Prof. Abelard Samothrace, of Columbia University, probably would have admitted that just as the two had lived in the same house—albeit at different levels—on Fifth Avenue, so their forebears at some prehistoric period had, likely as not, occupied the same cave and had in company waded on frosty mornings the ice-skimmed swamps of Mittel Europa in pursuit of the cave bear, the mastodon and the woolly rhinoceros, and for afternoon relaxation had made up twosomes for hunting wives with stone clubs instead of mashies in their hairy prehensile hands.

It would seem, therefore, that—whatever of tradition might have originated in the epoch in question—glimmerings of sportsmanship, of personal pride, of tribal duty or of conscience ought to have been the common heritage of them both. For it was assuredly true that while Miss Katie's historic ancestors had been Celtiberians, clad on occasion only in a thin coating of blue paint, Miss Althea's had dwelt in the dank marshes of the Elbe and had been unmistakably Teutonic, though this curse had been largely removed by racial intermarriage during subsequent thousands of years. Indeed, it may well have been that in the dimmer past some Beekman serf on bended knee had handed a gilded harp to some King O'Connell on his throne. If the O'Connells were foreigners the Beekmans, from the point of view of the aboriginal American, were no less so simply because they had preceded them by a couple of hundred years.

Tradition is not a matter of centuries but of ages. If Katie inherited some of hers from the peat bogs adjacent to Tara's Halls in that remote period when there were still snakes in Ireland, Miss Althea had vicariously acquired others from the fur-clad barbarians described by Tacitus who spent their leisure time in drinking, gambling or splitting each other's skulls with stone mallets. On this subject see Spencer's "Data of Ethics" and Lecky's "History of European Morals." But all this entirely escaped Miss Althea, who suffered from the erroneous impression that because she was a Beekman and lived in a stone mansion facing Central Park she differed fundamentally not only from the O'Connells but from the Smiths, the Pasquales, the Ivanovitches and the Ginsbergs, all of whom really come of very old families. Upon this supposed difference she prided herself.

Because she was, in fact, mistaken and because the O'Connells shared with the Beekmans and the Ginsbergs a tradition reaching back to a period when revenge was justice, and custom of kinsfolk the only law, Shane O'Connell had sought out Red McGurk and had sent him unshriven to his God. The only reason why this everyday Bowery occurrence excited any particular attention was not that Shane was an O'Connell but that McGurk was the son of a political boss of much influence and himself one of the leaders of a notorious cohort of young ruffians who when necessary could be relied upon to stuff a ballot box or otherwise to influence public opinion. As Red was a mighty man in Gideon, so his taking off was an event of moment, and he was waked with an elegance unsurpassed in the annals of Cherry Hill.

"An' if ye don't put the son-of-a——- who kilt me b'y in th' chair, ye name's mud—see?" the elder McGurk had informed District Attorney Peckham the next morning. "I've told the cops who done it. Now you do the rest—understand?"

Peckham understood very well. No one seeing the expression on McGurk's purple countenance could have failed to do so.

"We'll get him! Don't you worry!" Peckham had assured the desolated father with a manner subtly suggesting both the profoundest sympathy and the prophetic glories of a juridical revenge in which the name of McGurk would be upon every lip and the picture of the deceased, his family, and the home in which they dwelt would be featured on the front page of every journal. "We'll get him, all right!"

"See to it that ye do!" commented his visitor meaningly.

Therefore, though no one had seen him commit the crime, word was passed along the line to pick up Shane O'Connell for the murder of Red McGurk. It mattered not there was no evidence except the report of a muttered threat or two and the lie passed openly the week before.

Everybody knew that Shane had done it, and why; though no one could tell how he knew it. And because everybody knew, it became a political necessity for Peckham to put him under arrest with a great fanfare of trumpets and a grandiose announcement of the celerity with which the current would be turned through his body.

The only fly in the ointment was the fact that O'Connell had walked into the district attorney's office as soon as the rumor reached him and quietly submitted to being arrested, saying merely: "I heard you wanted me. Well, here I am!"

But though they badgered him for hours, lured him by every pretext to confess, put a stool pigeon in the same cell with him, and resorted to every trick, device and expedient known to the prosecutor's office to trap him into some sort of an admission, they got nothing for their pains. It was just one of those cases where the evidence simply wasn't forthcoming. And yet Peckham was aware that unless he convicted O'Connell his name would indeed be mud—or worse. This story, however, is concerned less with the family honor of the O'Connells than with that of the Beekmans.

Miss Althea was the last surviving member of her branch of the family. Though she would probably have regarded it as slightly vulgar to have been referred to as "one hundred per cent American" she was so nearly so—except for a reminiscent affection for "the late dear Queen"—that the phrase in her case would have been substantially correct. Her mother had been the daughter of a distinguished Revolutionary statesman who had been a signer of the Declaration of Independence, an ambassador and justice of the Supreme Court as well; her father a celebrated newspaper editor.

She had been born in the Prue and I period in Gramercy Park near what is now The Players' Club, and the old colonial house with its white trimmings and ornamental ironwork had been the scene of many a modest gayety at a time when Emerson, Lowell, and George William Curtis were viewed less as citizens than as high priests of Culture, sharing equally in sanctity with the goddess thereof. She could just remember those benign old gentlemen, as well as the many veterans of the Civil War who dined at her father's decorous mahogany and talked of the preservation of the Constitution and those other institutions to found which it is generally assumed the first settlers landed on the Atlantic seaboard and self-sacrificingly accepted real estate from the wily native in return for whisky and glass beads. She was forty-seven years of age, a Colonial Dame, a Daughter of the American Revolution, a member of the board of directors of several charitable institutions, and she was worth a couple of million dollars in railroad securities. On Sundays she always attended the church in Stuyvesant Square frequented by her family, and as late as 1907 did so in the famous Beekman C-spring victoria driven by an aged negro coachman.

But besides being full of rectitude and good works—which of themselves so often fail of attraction—Miss Althea was possessed of a face so charming even in its slightly faded prettiness that one wondered how it was possible that she could successfully have withstood the suitors who must have crowded about her. Her house on Fifth Avenue was full of old engravings of American patriots, and the library inherited from her editorial parent was replete with volumes upon subjects which would have filled a Bolshevik with disgust. Briefly, if ever Trotzky had become Commissar of the Soviet of Manhattan, Miss Althea and those like her would have been the first candidates for a drumhead court-martial.

She prided herself equally upon her adherence to religious principle and the Acts of Congress. For the law, merely as law, she had the profoundest veneration, viewing the heterogeneous statutes passed from time to time by desultory legislators much as if they had in some mysterious way been handed down from Mount Sinai along with the Ten Commandments.

For any violator of the law she had the uttermost abhorrence, and the only weakness in her ethics arose out of her failure to discriminate between relative importances, for she undoubtedly regarded the sale of a glass of beer after the closing hour as being quite as reprehensible as grand larceny or the bearing of false witness. To her every judge must be a learned, wise and honorable man because he stood for the enforcement of the law of the land, and she never questioned whether or not that law was wise or otherwise, which latter often—it must be confessed—it was not.

In a word, though there was nothing progressive about Miss Althea she was one of those delightful, cultivated, loyal and enthusiastic female citizens who are rightfully regarded as vertebrae in the backbone of a country which, after it has got its back up, can undoubtedly lick any other nation on earth. It was characteristic of her that carefully folded inside the will drawn for her by her family solicitor was a slip of paper addressed to her heirs and next of kin requesting that at her funeral the national anthem should be played and that her coffin should be draped with the American flag.

But there was a somewhat curious if not uncommon inconsistency in Miss Beekman's attitude toward lawbreakers in that once they were in prison they instantly became objects of her gentlest solicitude. Thus she was a frequent visitor at the Tombs, where she brought spiritual, and more often, it must be frankly admitted, bodily comfort to those of the inmates who were recommended by the district attorney and prison authorities as worthy of her attention; and Prosecutor Peckham being not unmindful of the possible political advantage that might accrue from being on friendly terms with so well-known a member of the distinguished family of Beekman, lost no opportunity to ingratiate himself with her and gave orders, to his subordinates to make her path as easy as possible. Thus quite naturally she had heard of Tutt & Tutt, and had a casual acquaintance with the senior partner himself.

"That O'Connell is a regular clam—won't tell me anything at all!" remarked Mr. Tutt severely, hanging up his hat on the office tree with one hand while he felt for a match in his waistcoat pocket with the other, upon the afternoon of the day that Miss Beekman had had the conversation with Dawkins with which this story opens.

"National temperament," answered Bonnie Doon, producing the desired match. "It's just like an Irishman to refuse point-blank to talk to the lawyer who has been assigned to defend him. He's probably afraid he'll make some admission from which you will infer he's guilty. No Irishman ever yet admitted that he was guilty of anything!"

"Well, I've never met a defendant of any other nationality who would, either," replied Mr. Tutt, pulling vigorously at his stogy. "Even so, this chap O'Connell is a puzzle to me. 'Go ahead and defend me,' said he today, 'but don't ask me to talk about the case, because I won't.' I give it up. He wouldn't even tell me where he was on the day of the murder."

Bonnie grunted dubiously.

"There may be a very good reason for that!" he retorted. "If what rumor says is true he simply hunted for McGurk until he found him and put a lead pellet back of his ear."

"And also, if what rumor says is true," supplemented Tutt, who entered at this moment, "a good job it was, too. McGurk was a treacherous, dirty blackguard, the leader of a gang of criminals, even if he was, as they all agree, a handsome rascal who had every woman in the district on tenterhooks. Any girl in this case?"

Bonnie shrugged his shoulders.

"They claim so; only there's nothing definite. The O'Connells are well spoken of."

"If there was, that would explain why he wouldn't talk," commented Mr. Tutt. "That's the devil of it. You can't put in a defense under the unwritten law without besmirching the very reputation you are trying to protect."

The senior partner of Tutt & Tutt wheeled his swivel chair to the window and crossing his congress boots upon the sill gazed contemplatively down upon the shipping.

"Unwritten law!" sarcastically exclaimed Tutt from the doorway. "There ain't no such animal in these parts!"

"You're quite wrong!" retorted his elder partner. "Most of our law—ninety-nine per cent of it, in fact—is unwritten."

"Excuse me!" interjected Bonnie Doon, abandoning his usual flippancy. "What is that you said, Mr. Tutt?"

"That ninety-nine per cent of the laws by which we are governed are unwritten laws, just as binding as the printed ones upon our statute books, which after all are only the crystallization of the sentiments and opinions of the community based upon its traditions, manners, customs and religious beliefs. For every statute in print there are a hundred that have no tangible existence, based on our sense of decency, of duty and of honor, which are equally controlling and which it has never been found necessary to reduce to writing, since their infraction usually brings its own penalty or infringes the more delicate domain of private conscience where the crude processes of the criminal law cannot follow. The laws of etiquette and fair play are just as obligatory as legislative enactments—the Ten Commandments as efficacious as the Penal Code."

"Don't you agree with that, Tutt?" demanded Bonnie. "Every man's conscience is his own private unwritten law."

Tutt looked skeptical.

"Did you say every man had a conscience?" he inquired.

"And it makes a lot of trouble sometimes," continued Mr. Tutt, ignoring him. "You remember when old Cogswell was on the bench and a man was brought before him for breaking his umbrella over the head of a fellow who had insulted the defendant's wife, he said to the jury: 'Gentlemen, if this plaintiff had called my wife a name like that I'd have smashed my umbrella over his head pretty quick. However, that's not the law! Take the case, gentlemen!'"

"Well, I guess I was wrong," admitted Tutt. "Of course, that is unwritten law. People don't like to punish a man for resenting a slur upon his wife's reputation."

"But you see where that leads you?" remarked his partner. "The so-called unwritten law is based on our inherited idea of chivalry. A lady's honor and reputation were sacred, and her knight was prepared instantly to defend it with the last drop of his blood. A reflection on her honesty was almost as unbearable as one upon her virtue. Logically, the unwritten law ought to permit women to break their contracts and do practically anything they see fit."

"They do, don't they—the dear things!" sighed Bonnie.

"I remember," interjected Tutt brightly, "when it was the unwritten law of Cook County, Illinois—that's Chicago, you know—that any woman could kill her husband for the life-insurance money. Seriously!"

"There's no point of chivalry that I can see involved in that—it's merely good business," remarked Mr. Doon, lighting another cigarette. "All the same it's obvious that the unwritten law might be stretched a long way. It's a great convenience, though, on occasion!"

"We should be in an awful stew if nowadays we substituted ideas of chivalry for those of justice," declared Mr. Tutt. "Fortunately the danger is past. As someone has said, 'The women, once our superiors, have become our equals!'"

"We don't even give 'em our seats in the Subway," commented Tutt complacently. "No, we needn't worry about the return of chivalry—in New York at any rate."

"I should say not!" exclaimed Miss Wiggin, entering at that moment with a pile of papers, as nobody rose.

"But," insisted Bonnie, "all the same there are certainly plenty of cases where if he had to choose between them any man would obey his conscience rather than the law."

"Of course, there are such cases," admitted Mr. Tutt. "But we ought to discourage the idea as much as possible."

"Discourage a sense of honor?" exclaimed Miss Wiggin. "Why, Mr. Tutt!"

"It depends on what you mean by honor," he retorted. "I don't take much stock in the kind of honor that makes an heir apparent 'perjure himself like a gentleman' about a card game at a country house."

"Neither do I," she returned, "any more than I do in the kind of honor that compels a man to pay a gambling debt before he pays his tailor, but I do believe that there may be situations where, though it would not be permissible to perjure oneself, honor would require one to refuse to obey the law."

"That's a pretty dangerous doctrine," reflected Mr. Tutt. "For everybody would be free to make himself the judge of when he ought to respect the law and when he oughtn't. We can easily imagine that the law would come out at the small end of the horn."

"In matters of conscience—which, I take it, is the same thing as one's sense of honor—one has got to be one's own judge," declared Miss Wiggin firmly.

"The simplest way," announced Tutt, "is to take the position that the law should always be obeyed and that the most honorable man is he who respects it the most."

"Yes, the safest and also the most cowardly!" retorted Miss Wiggin. "Supposing the law required you to do something which you personally regarded not only as morally wrong but detestable, would you do it?"

"It wouldn't!" protested Tutt with a grimace. "The law is the perfection of reason."

"But I am entitled, am I not, to suppose, for purposes of argument, that it might?" she inquired caustically. "And I say that our sense of honor is the most precious thing we've got. It's our duty to respect our institutions and obey the law whether we like it or not, unless it conflicts with our conscience, in which case we ought to defy it and take the consequences!"

"Dear me!" mocked Tutt. "And be burned at the stake?"

"If necessary; yes!"

"I don't rightly get all this!" remarked Bonnie. "Me for the lee side of the law, every time!"

"It's highly theoretical," commented Tutt. "As usual with our discussions."

"Not so theoretical as you might think!" interrupted his senior, hastening to reenforce Miss Wiggin. "Nobody can deny that to be true to oneself is the highest principle of human conduct, and that "tis man's perdition to be safe when for the truth he ought to die.' That's why we reverence the early Christian martyrs. But when it comes to choosing between what we loosely call honor and what the law requires—"

"But I thought the law embodied our ideas of honor!" replied Tutt. "Didn't you say so—a few hours earlier in this conversation? As our highest duty is to the state, it is a mere play on words, in my humble opinion, to speak of honor as distinguished from law or the obligation of one's oath in a court of justice. I bet I can find plenty of authorities to that effect in the library!"

"Of course you can," countered Miss Wiggin. "You can find an authority on any side of any proposition you want to look for. That's why one's own sense of honor is so much more reliable than the law. What is the law, anyhow? It's what some judge says is the law—until he's reversed. Do you suppose I'd surrender my own private ideas of honor to a casual ruling from a judge who very likely hadn't the remotest idea of what I think is honorable?"

"You'll be jailed for contempt before you get through!" Tutt warned her.

"The fact of the matter is," concluded Mr. Tutt, "that honor and law haven't anything to do with one another. The courts have constantly pointed that out from the earliest days, though judges like, when they can, to make the two seem one and the same. Chief Baron Bowes, I remember, said in some case in 1743, 'The court can't determine what is honor.' No, no; the two are different, and that difference will always make trouble. Isn't it nearly tea time?"

Miss Beekman was just stepping off the elevator on the first floor of the Tombs the next afternoon on one of her weekly visits when she came face to face with Mr. Tutt.

She greeted him cordially, for she had taken rather a fancy to the shabby old man, drawn to him, in spite of her natural aversion to all members of the criminal bar, by the gentle refinement of his weather-beaten face. "I hope you have had a successful day."

The lawyer shook his head in a pseudo-melancholy manner.

"Unfortunately, I have not," he answered whimsically. "My only client refuses to speak to me! Perhaps you could get something out of him for me."

"Oh, they all talk to me readily enough!" she replied. "I fancy they know I'm harmless. What is his name?"

"Shane O'Connell."

"What is his offense?"

"He is charged with murder."

"Oh!"

Miss Althea recoiled. Her charitable impulses did not extend to defendants charged with homicide. There was too much notoriety connected with them, for one thing; there was nothing she hated so much as notoriety.

"Seriously," he went on with earnestness, "I wish you'd have a word with him. It's pretty hard to have to defend a man and not to know a thing about his side of the case. It's almost your duty, don't you think?"

Miss Althea hesitated, and was lost.

"Very well," she answered reluctantly, "I'll see what I can do. Perhaps he needs some medicine or letter paper or something. I'll get an order from the warden and go right back and see him."

Twenty minutes later Shane O'Connell faced Miss Beekman sullenly across the deal table of the counsel room. A ray of late sunshine fell through the high grating of the heavily barred window upon a face quite different from those which Miss Althea was accustomed to encounter in these surroundings, for it showed no touch of depravity or evil habits, and confinement had not yet deprived its cheeks of their rugged mantle of crimson or its eyes of their bold gleam.

He was little more than a boy, this murderer, as handsome a lad as ever swaggered out of County Kerry.

"An' what may it be that leads you to send for such as me, Miss Beekman!" he demanded, glowering at her.

She felt suddenly unnerved, startled and rather shocked at his use of her name. Where could he have discovered it? From the keeper, probably, she decided. All her usual composure, her quiet self-possession, her aloof and slightly condescending sweetness—had deserted her.

"I thought," she stammered—"I might—possibly—be of help to you."

"'Tis too late to make up for the harm ye've done!" His coal-black eyes reached into her shrinking body as if to tear out her heart.

"I!" she gasped. "I—do harm! What do you mean?"

"Did not my sister Katie work for yez?" he asked, and his words leaped and curled about her like hissing flames. "Did you see after her or watch her comings and goings, as she saw after you—she a mere lass of sixteen? Arrah! No!"

With a sensation of horror Miss Althea realized that at last she was in a murder case in spite of herself! This lad, the brother of Katie, the waitress whom she had discharged! How curious! And how unfortunate! His charge was preposterous; nevertheless a faint blush stole to her cheek and she looked away.

"How ridiculous!" she managed to say. "It was no part of my obligation to look after her! How could I?"

His hawk's eyes watched her every tremor.

"Did ye not lock her out the night of the ball when she went wid McGurk?"

"I—how absurd!"

Suddenly she faltered. An indistinct accusing recollection turned her faint—of the housekeeper having told her that one of the girls insisted on going to a dance on an evening not hers by arrangement, and how she had given orders that the house should be closed the same as usual at ten o'clock for the night. If the girl couldn't abide by the rules of the Beekman ménage she could sleep somewhere else. What of it? Supposing she had done so? She could not be held responsible for remote, unreasonable and discreditable consequences!

And then by chance Shane O'Connell made use of a phrase that indirectly saved his life, a phrase curiously like the one used on a former occasion by Dawkins to Miss Althea:

"Katie was a member of your household; ye might have had a bit of thought for her!" he asserted bitterly.

Dawkins had said: "You'd think a girl would have some consideration for her employer, if nothing else. In a sense she is a guest in the house and should behave herself as such."

There was no sense in it! There was no parallel, no analogy. There was no obligation to treat the girl as a guest, even though the girl should have acted like one. Miss Beekman knew it. And yet there was—something! Didn't she owe some sort of duty at any rate toward those in her employment—those who slept under her roof?

"'Twould have been better to have been kind to her then than to be kind to me now!" said he with sad conviction.

The proud Miss Althea Beekman, the dignified descendant of a long line of ancestors, turned red. Heretofore serenely confident of her own personal virtue and her own artificial standards of democracy, she now found herself humiliated and chagrined before this rough young criminal.

"You—are—quite right!" she confessed, her eyes smarting with sudden tears. "My position is quite—quite illogical. But of course I had no idea! Please, please let me try to help you—if I can—and Katie, too—if it isn't too late."

Shane O'Connell experienced contrition. After all it was not seemly that the likes of him should be dictating to the likes of her. And he could never abide seeing a woman—particularly a pretty woman—cry.

"Forgive me, madam!" he begged, lowering his head.

"You were quite justified in all you said!" she assured him. "Please tell me everything that has happened. I have influence with the district attorney and—in other places. No doubt I can be of assistance to you. Of course, you can absolutely trust me!"

Shane O'Connell, looking into her honest gray eyes, knew that he could trust her. Slowly—brokenly—tensely, he told her how he had killed Red McGurk, and why.

The corridors were full of shadows when Althea Beekman put her hands on Shane O'Connell's shoulders and bade him good night. Though she abominated his crime and loathed him for having committed it she felt in some way partially responsible, and she also perceived that, by the code of the O'Connells, Shane had done what he believed to be right. He had taken the law into his own hands and he was ready to pay the necessary penalty. He would have done the same thing all over again. To this extent at least he had her respect.

She found Mr. Tutt waiting for her on the bench by the warden's office.

"Well?" he asked with a smile, rising to greet her and tossing away his stogy.

"I haven't very good news for you," she answered regretfully. "He's confessed to me—told me everything—why he shot him and where he bought the pistol. He's a brave boy, though! It's a sad case! But what can you do with people who believe themselves justified in doing things like that?"

She did not notice Detective Eddie Conroy, of the D.A.'s office, standing behind an adjacent pillar, ostentatiously lighting a cigar; nor see him smile as he slowly walked away.

"Talk about luck!" exulted O'Brien, the yellow dog of the district attorney's office, an hour later to his chief. "What do you think, boss? Eddie Conroy heard Miss Beekman telling old man Tutt over in the Tombs that O'Connell had confessed to her! Say, how's that? Some evidence—what?"

"What good will that do us?" asked Peckham, glancing up with a scowl from his desk. "She won't testify for us."

"But she'll have to testify if we call her, won't she?" demanded his assistant.

The district attorney drummed on the polished surface before him.

"We—ell, I suppose so," he admitted hesitatingly. "But you can't just subpoena a woman like that without any warning and put her on the stand and make her testify. It would be too rough!"

"It's the only way to do it!" retorted O'Brien with a sly grin. "If she knew in advance that we were thinking of calling her she'd beat it out of town."

"That's true," agreed his chief. "That's as far as she'd go, too, in defying the law. But I don't much like it. Those Beekmans have a lot of influence, and if she got sore she could make us a heap of trouble! Besides it's sort of a scaly trick making her give up on him like that."

O'Brien raised his brows.

"Scaly trick! He's a murderer, isn't he? And he'll get off if we don't call her. It's a matter of duty, as I see it."

"All the same, my son, your suggestion has a rotten smell to it. We may have to do it—I don't say we won't—but it's risky business!" replied Peckham dubiously.

"It's a good deal less risky than not doing it, so far as your candidacy next autumn is concerned!" retorted his assistant. "We won't let her suspect what we're goin' to do; and the last minute I'll call her to the stand and cinch the case!

She won't even know who called her! Perhaps I can arrange with Judge Babson to call her on some other point and then pretend to sort of stumble onto the fact of the confession and examine her himself. That would let us out. I can smear it over somehow."

"You'd better," commented Peckham, "unless you want a howl from the papers! It would make quite a story if Miss Althea Beekman got on the rampage. She could have your scalp, my boy, if she wanted it!"

"And McGurk could have yours!" retorted O'Brien with the impudence born of knowledge.

The prosecution of Shane O'Connell, which otherwise might have slowly languished and languishing died, took on new life owing to the evidence thus innocently delivered into the hands of the district attorney; in fact it became a *cause célèbre*. The essential elements to convict were now all there—the *corpus delicti*, evidence of threats on the part of the defendant, of motive, of opportunity, and—his confession. The law which provides that the statement of an accused "is not sufficient to warrant his conviction without additional proof that the crime charged has been committed" would be abundantly satisfied—though without his confession there would have been no proof whatever that the crime charged had been committed by him.

Thus, without her knowing it, Miss Beekman was an essential witness and, in fact, the pivot upon which the entire case turned.

The day of the great sporting event came. With it arrived in full panoply the McGurks, their relatives and followers. All Cherry Hill seemed to have packed itself into Part I of the Supreme Court. There was an atmosphere somehow suggestive of the races or a prize fight. But it was a sporting event which savored of a sure thing—really more like a hanging. They were there to make holiday over the law's revenge for the killing of the darling of the Pearl Button Kids. Peckham personally assured McGurk that everything was copper-fastened.

"He's halfway up the river already!" he said jocularly.

And McGurk, swelling with importance and emotion, pulled a couple of cigars from his pocket and the two smoked the pipe of peace.

But the reader is not particularly concerned with the progress of the trial, for he has already attended many. It is enough to say that a jury with undershot jaws, who had proved by previous experience their indifference to capital punishment and to all human sympathy, were finally selected and that the witnesses were duly called, and testified to the usual facts, while the Pearl Button Kids and the rest, spitting surreptitiously beneath the benches, eagerly drank in every word. There was nothing for Mr. Tutt to do; nothing for him to deny. The case built itself up, brick by brick. And Shane O'Connell sat there unemotionally, hardly listening. There was nothing in the evidence to reflect in any way upon the honor of the O'Connells in general or in particular. He had done that which that honor demanded and he was ready to pay the penalty—if the law could get him. He assumed that it would get him. So did the Tutts.

But when toward the end of the third day nothing had yet been brought forward to connect him with the crime Tutt leaned over and whispered to Mr. Tutt, "D'ye know, I'm beginning to have a hunch there isn't any case!"

Mr. Tutt made an imperceptible gesture of assent.

"Looks that way," he answered out of the corner of his mouth. "Probably they'll spring the connecting evidence at the end and give us the *coup de grâce*."

At that moment a police witness was released from the stand and O'Brien stepped to the bench and whispered something to the judge, who glanced at the clock and nodded. It was twenty minutes of four, and the jury were already getting restless, for the trial had developed into a humdrum, cut-and-dried affair.

Miss Beekman sitting far back in the rear of the court room suddenly heard O'Brien call her name, and a quiver of apprehension passed through her body. She had never testified in any legal proceeding, and the idea of getting up before such a crowd of people and answering questions filled her with dismay. It was so public! Still, if it was going to help O'Connell—

"Althea Beekman," bellowed Cap. Phelan, "to the witness chair!"

Althea Beekman! The gentle lady felt as if she had been rudely stripped of all her protective clothing. Althea! Did not the law do her the courtesy of calling her even "Miss"? Nerving herself to the performance of her duty she falteringly made her way between the crowded benches, past the reporters' table, and round back of the jury box. The judge, apparently a pleasant-faced, rather elderly man, bowed gravely to her, indicated where she should sit and administered the oath to her himself, subtly dwelling upon the phrase "the whole truth," and raising his eyes heavenward as he solemnly pronounced the words "so help you God!"

"I do!" declared Miss Beekman primly but decidedly.

Behind her upon the court-room wall towered in its flowing draperies the majestic figure of the Goddess of the Law, blindfolded and holding aloft the scales of justice. Beside her sat in the silken robes of his sacred office a judge who cleverly administered that law to advance his own interests and those of his political associates. In front of her, treacherously smiling, stood the cynical, bullet-headed O'Brien. At a great distance Mr. Tutt leaned on his elbows at a table beside Shane O'Connell. To them she directed her gaze and faintly smiled.

"Miss Beekman," began O'Brien as courteously as he knew how, "you reside, do you not, at Number 1000 Fifth Avenue, in this city and county?"

"I do," she answered with resolution.

"Your family have always lived in New York, have they not?"

"Since 1630," she replied deprecatingly and with more confidence.

"You are prominent in various philanthropic, religious and civic activities?"

"Not prominent; interested," she corrected him.

"And you make a practise of visiting prisoners in the Tombs?"

She hesitated. What could this be leading to?

"Occasionally," she admitted.

"Do you know this defendant, Shane O'Connell?"

"Yes."

"Did you see him on the twenty-third day of last month?"

"I think so—if that was the day."

"What day do you refer to?"

"The day I had the talk with him."

"Oh, you had a talk with him?"

"Yes."

"Where did you have that talk with him?"

"In the counsel room of the Tombs."

O'Brien paused. Even his miserable soul revolted at what he was about to do. "What did he say?" he asked, nervously looking away.

Something in his hangdog look warned Miss Beekman that she was being betrayed, but before she could answer Mr. Tutt was on his feet.

"One moment!" he cried. "May I ask a preliminary question?"

The court signified acquiescence.

"Was that conversation which you had with the defendant a confidential one?"

"I object to the question!" snapped O'Brien. "The law recognizes no confidential communications as privileged except those made to a priest, a physician or an attorney. The witness is none of these. The question is immaterial and irrelevant."

"That is the law," announced the judge, "but under all the circumstances I will permit the witness to answer."

Miss Beekman paused.

"Why," she began, "of course it was confidential, Mr. Tutt. O'Connell wouldn't have told me anything if he had supposed for one moment I was going to repeat what he said. Besides, I suggested that I might be able to help him. Yes, certainly our talk was confidential."

"I am sorry," gloated O'Brien, "but I shall have to ask you what it was."

"That is not a question," said Mr. Tutt calmly.

"What did the defendant say to you in the counsel room of the Tombs on the twenty-third of last month?" cautiously revised O'Brien.

"I object!" thundered Mr. Tutt, his form towering until seemingly it matched that of the blind goddess in height. "I object to the answer as requiring a breach of confidence which the law could not tolerate."

Judge Babson turned politely to Miss Beekman.

"I regret very much that I shall be obliged to ask you to state what the defendant said to you. You will recall that you yourself volunteered the information that you had had the talk in question. Otherwise"—he coughed and put up his hand—"we might possibly never have learned of it. A defendant cannot deprive the people of the right to prove what he may have divulged respecting his offense merely by claiming that it was in confidence. Public policy could never allow that. It may be unpleasant for you to answer the question but I must ask you to do so."

"But," she protested, "you certainly cannot expect me to betray a confidence! I asked O'Connell to tell me what he had done so that I could help him—and he trusted me!"

"But you are not responsible for the law! He took his chance!" admonished the judge.

Slowly Miss Althea's indignation rose as she perceived the dastardly trick which O'Brien had played upon her. Already she suspected that the judge was only masquerading in the clothing of a gentleman. With a white face she turned to Mr. Tutt.

"Does the law require me to answer, Mr. Tutt?" she inquired.

"Do not ask questions—answer them," ordered Babson brusquely, feeling the change in her manner. "You are a witness for the people—not the defendant."

"I am not a witness against O'Connell!" she declared. "This man"—indicating O'Brien scornfully—"has in some way found out that I—Oh, surely the law doesn't demand anything so base as that!"

There was silence. The wheels of justice hung on a dead center.

"Answer the question," remarked His Honor tartly.

All Miss Beekman's long line of ancestors turned in their graves. In her Beekman blood the chief justice, the ambassador, the great editor, the signer of the Declaration of Independence, stirred, awoke, rubbed their eyes and sternly reared themselves. And that blood—blue though it was instead of scarlet like the O'Connells'—boiled in her veins and burned through the delicate tissue of her cheeks.

"My conscience will not permit me to betray a confidence!" she cried angrily.

"I direct you to answer!" ordered the judge.

"I object to the court's threatening the witness!" interjected Mr. Tutt. "I wish it to appear upon the record that the manner of the court is most unjudicial and damaging to the defendant."

"Take your seat, sir!" barked Babson, his features swelling with anger. "Your language is contemptuous!"

The jury were leaning forward intently. Trained militiamen of the gibbet, they nevertheless admired this little woman's fearlessness and the old lawyer's pugnacity. On the rear wall the yellow face of the old self-regulating clock, that had gayly ticked so many men into the electric chair, leered shamelessly across at the blind goddess.

"Answer the question, madam! If, as you claim, you are a patriotic citizen of this commonwealth, having due respect for its institutions and for the statutes, you will not set up your own ideas of what the law ought to be in defiance of the law as it stands. I order you to answer! If you do not I shall be obliged to take steps to compel you to do so."

In the dead silence that followed, the stones in the edifice of Miss Beekman's inherited complacency, with each beat of the clock, fell one by one to the ground until it was entirely demolished. Vainly she struggled to test her conscience by her loyalty to her country's laws. But the task was beyond her.

Tightly compressing her lips she sat silent in the chair, while the delighted reporters scribbled furious messages to their city editors that Miss Althea Beekman, one of the Four Hundred, was defying Judge Babson, and to rush up a camera man right off in a taxi, and to look her up in the morgue for a front-page story. O'Brien glanced uneasily at Babson. Possible defiance on the part of this usually unassuming lady had not entered into his calculations. The judge took a new tack.

"You probably do not fully understand the situation in which you are placed," he explained. "You are not responsible for the law. Neither are you responsible in any way for the consequences to this defendant, whatever they may be. The matter is entirely out of your hands. You are compelled to do as the court orders. As a law-abiding citizen you have no choice in the matter."

Miss Althea's modest intellect reeled, but she stood her ground, the ghost of the Signer at her elbow.

"I am sorry," she replied, "but my own self-respect will not allow me to answer."

"In that case," declared Babson, playing his trump card, "it will be my unpleasant duty to commit you for contempt."

There was a bustle of excitement about the reporters' table. Here was a story!

"Very well," answered Miss Beekman proudly. "Do as you see fit, and as your own duty and conscience demand."

The judge could not conceal his annoyance. The last thing in the world that he wished to do was to send Miss Althea to jail. But having threatened her he must carry out his threat or forever lose face.

"I will give the witness until tomorrow morning at half after ten o'clock to make up her mind what she will do," he announced after a hurried conference with O'Brien. "Adjourn court!"

Miss Beekman did not go to bed at all that night. Until a late hour she conferred in the secrecy of her Fifth Avenue library with her gray-haired solicitor, who, in some mysterious way, merely over the telephone, managed to induce the newspapers to omit any reference to his client's contemptuous conduct in their morning editions.

"There's no way out of it, my dear," he said finally as he took his leave—he was her father's cousin and very fond of her—"this judge has the power to send you to jail if he wants to—and dares to! It's an even chance whether he will dare to or not. It depends on whether he prefers to stand well with the McGurks or with the general public. Of course I respect your attitude, but really I think you are a little quixotic. Points of honor are too ephemeral to be debated in courts of justice. To do so would be to open the door to all kinds of abuses. Dishonest witnesses would constantly avail themselves of the opportunity to avoid giving evidence."

"Dishonest witnesses would probably lie in the first place!" she quavered.

"True! I quite overlooked that!" he smiled, gazing down at her in an avuncular manner. "But to-day the question isn't open. It is settled, whether we like it or not. No pledge of privacy, no oath of secrecy—can avail against demand in a court of justice. Even confessions obtained by fraud are admissible—though we might wish otherwise."

Miss Beekman shrugged her shoulders.

"Nothing you have said seems to me to alter the situation."

"Very well," he replied. "I guess that settles it. Knowing you and the Beekman breed! There's one thing I must say," he added as he stood in the doorway after bidding her good night—"that old fellow Tutt has behaved pretty well, leaving you entirely alone this way. I always had an idea he was a sort of shyster. Most attorneys of that class would have been sitting on your doorstep all the evening trying to persuade you to stick to your resolution not to give their client away, and to do the square thing. But he's done nothing of the sort. Rather decent on the whole!"

"Perhaps he recognizes a woman of honor when he sees one!" she retorted.

"Honor!" he muttered as he closed the door. "What crimes are sometimes committed in thy name!"

But on the steps he stopped and looked back affectionately at the library window.

"After all, Althea's a good sport!" he remarked to himself.

At or about the same moment a quite dissimilar conference was being held between Judge Babson and Assistant District Attorney O'Brien in the café of the Passamaquoddy Club.

"She'll cave!" declared O'Brien, draining his glass. "Holy Mike! No woman like her is going to stay in jail! Besides, if you don't commit her everybody will say that you were scared to—yielded to influence. You're in the right and it will be a big card for you to show that you aren't afraid of anybody!"

Babson pulled nervously on his cigar.

"Maybe that's so," he said, "but I don't much fancy an appellate court sustaining me on the law and at the same time roasting hell out of me as a man!"

"Oh, they won't do that!" protested O'Brien. "How could they? All they're interested in is the law!"

"I've known those fellows to do queer things sometimes," answered the learned judge. "And the Beekmans are pretty powerful people."

"Well, so are the McGurks!" warned O'Brien.

"Now, Miss Beekman," said Judge Babson most genially the next morning, after that lady had taken her seat in the witness chair and the jury had answered to their names, "I hope you feel differently to-day about giving your testimony. Don't you think that after all it would be more fitting if you answered the question?"

Miss Althea firmly compressed her lips.

"At least let me read you some of the law on the subject," continued His Honor patiently. "Originally many people, like yourself, had the mistaken idea that what they called their honor should be allowed to intervene between them and their duty. And even the courts sometimes so held. But that was long ago—in the sixteenth and seventeenth centuries. To-day the law wisely recognizes no such thing. Let me read you what Baron Hotham said, in Hill's Trial in 1777, respecting the testimony of a witness who very properly told the court what the accused had said to him. It is very clearly put:

"'The defendant certainly thought him his friend, and he'—the defendant—'therefore did disclose all this to him. Gentlemen, one has only to say further that if this point of honor was to be so sacred as that a man who comes by knowledge of this sort from an offender was not to be at liberty to disclose it the most atrocious criminals would every day escape punishment; and therefore it is that the wisdom of the law knows nothing of that point of honor.'"

Miss Beekman listened politely.

By Advice of Counsel

"I am sorry," she replied with dignity. "I shall not change my mind. I refuse to answer the question, and—and you can do whatever you like with me."

"Do you understand that you are in contempt of this court? Do you intend to show contempt for this court?" he demanded wrathfully.

"I do," answered Miss Althea. "I have contempt for this court."

A titter danced along the benches and some fool in the back of the room clapped his hands.

Judge Babson's face grew hard and his eyes narrowed to steel points.

"The witness stands committed for contempt," he announced bitingly. "I direct that she be confined in the city prison for thirty days and pay a fine of two hundred and fifty dollars. Madam, you will go with the officer."

Miss Althea rose while the ghost of the Signer encircled her with his arm.

Mr. Tutt was already upon his feet. He knew that the ghost of the Signer was there.

"May I ask the court if the witness, having been committed for the contemptuous conduct of which she is obviously guilty, may remain in your chambers until adjournment, in order that she may arrange her private affairs?"

"I will grant her that privilege," agreed Judge Babson with internal relief. "The request is quite reasonable. Captain Phelan, you may take the witness into my robing room and keep her there for the present."

With her small head erect, her narrow shoulders thrown back, and with a resolute step as befitted the descendant of a long line of ancestors Miss Althea passed behind the jury box and disappeared.

The twelve looked at one another dubiously. Both Babson and O'Brien seemed nervous and undecided.

"Well, call your next witness," remarked the judge finally.

"But I haven't any more witnesses!" growled O'Brien. "And you know it almighty well, you idiot!" he muttered under his breath.

"If that is the people's case I move for the defendant's immediate discharge," cried Mr. Tutt, jumping to his feet. "There is no evidence connecting him with the crime."

McGurk, furious, sprang toward the bar.

"See here! Wait a minute! Hold on, judge! I can get a hundred witnesses—"

"Sit down!" shouted one of the officers, thrusting him back. "Keep quiet!"

Babson looked at O'Brien and elevated his forehead. Then as O'Brien gave a shrug the judge turned to the expectant jury and said in apologetic tones:

"Gentlemen of the jury, where the people have failed to prove the defendant's guilt beyond a reasonable doubt it is the duty of the court to direct a verdict. In this case, though by inference the testimony points strongly toward the prisoner, there is no direct proof against him and I am accordingly constrained—much as I regret it—to instruct you to return a verdict of not guilty."

In the confusion which followed the rendition of the verdict a messenger entered breathlessly and forcing his way through the crowd delivered a folded paper to Mr. Tutt, who immediately rose and handed it to the clerk; and that official, having hurriedly perused it and pursed his lips in surprise, passed it over the top of the bench to the judge.

"What's this?" demanded Babson. "Don't bother me now with trifles!"

"But it's a writ of habeas corpus, Your Honor, signed by Judge Winthrop, requiring the warden to produce Miss Beekman in Part I of the Supreme Court, and returnable forthwith," whispered Mr. McGuire in an awe-stricken voice. "I can't disregard that, you know!"

"What!" cried Babson. "How on earth could he have issued a writ in this space of time? The thing's impossible!"

"If Your Honor please," urbanely explained Mr. Tutt, "as—having known Miss Beekman's father—I anticipated that the witness would pursue the course of conduct which, in fact, she has, I prepared the necessary papers early this morning and as soon as you ordered her into custody my partner, who was waiting in Judge Winthrop's chambers, presented them to His Honor, secured his signature and brought the writ here in a taxicab."

Nobody seemed to be any longer interested in O'Connell. The reporters had left their places and pushed their way into the inclosure before the dais. In the rear of the room O'Brien was vainly engaged in trying to placate the Pearl Button Kids, who were loudly swearing vengeance upon both him and Peckham. It was a scene as nearly turbulent as the old yellow clock had ever witnessed. Even the court officers abandoned any effort to maintain order and joined the excited group about Mr. Tutt before the bench.

"Does Your Honor desire that this matter be argued before the Supreme Court?" inquired Mr. Tutt suavely. "If so I will ask that the prisoner be paroled in my custody. Judge Winthrop is waiting."

Babson had turned pale. Facing a dozen newspapermen, pencils in hand, he quailed. To hell with "face." Why, if he went on any longer with the farce the papers would roast the life out of him. With an apology for a smile that was, in fact, a ghastly grin, he addressed himself to the waiting group of jurymen, lawyers and reporters.

"Of course, gentlemen," he said, "I never had any real intention of dealing harshly with Miss Beekman. Undoubtedly she acted quite honestly and according to her best lights. She is a very estimable member of society. It will be unnecessary, Mr. Tutt, for you to argue the writ before Judge Winthrop. The relator, Althea Beekman, is discharged."

"Thank you, Your Honor!" returned Mr. Tutt, bowing profoundly, and lowering an eyelid in the direction of the gentlemen of the press. "You are indeed a wise and upright judge!"

The wise and upright judge rose grandly and gathered his robes about the judicial legs.

"Good morning, gentlemen," he remarked from his altitude to the reporters.

"Good morning, judge," they replied in chorus. "May we say anything about the writ?"

Judge Babson paused momentarily in his flight.

"Oh! Perhaps you might as well let the whole thing go," he answered carelessly. "On the whole I think it better that you should."

As they fought their way out of the doorway Charley Still, of the *Sun*, grinned at "Deacon" Terry, of the *Tribune*, and jocosely inquired: "Say, Deac., did you ever think why one calls a judge 'Your Honor'?"

The Deacon momentarily removed his elbow from the abdomen of the gentleman beside him and replied sincerely though breathlessly, "No! You can search me!"

And "Cap." Phelan, who happened to be setting his watch at just that instant, affirms that he will make affidavit that the old yellow clock winked across the room at the Goddess of Justice, and that beneath her bandages she unmistakably smiled.

By Advice of Counsel

"Kotow! Kotow! To the great Yen-How,
And wish him the longest of lives!
With his one-little, two-little, three-little, four-little,
Five-little, six-little wives!"

"The fact is I've been arrested for bigamy," said Mr. Higgleby in a pained and slightly resentful manner. He was an ample flabby person, built like an isosceles triangle with a smallish head for the apex, slightly expanded in the gangliar region just above the nape of the neck—medical students and phrenologists please note—and habitually wearing an expression of helpless pathos. Instinctively you felt that you wanted to do something for Mr. Higgleby—to mother him, maybe.

"Then you should see my partner, Mr. Tutt," said Mr. Tutt severely. "He's the matrimonial specialist."

"I want to see Mr. Tutt, the celebrated divorce lawyer," explained Mr. Higgleby.

"You mean my partner, Mr. Tutt," said Mr. Tutt. "Willie, show the gentleman in to Mr. Tutt."

"Thank you, sir," said Mr. Higgleby, and followed Willie.

"Is this Mr. Higgleby?" chirped Tutt as Higgleby entered the adjoining office. "Delighted to see you, sir! What can we—I—do for you?"

"The fact is, I've been arrested for bigamy," repeated Mr. Higgleby.

Now the Tutt system—demonstrated effective by years of experience—for putting a client in a properly grateful and hence liberal frame of mind was, like the method of some physicians, first to scare said client, or patient, out of his seven senses; second, to admit reluctantly, upon reflection, that in view of the fact that he had wisely come to Tutt & Tutt there might still be some hope for him; and third, to exculpate him with such a flourish of congratulation upon his escape that he was glad to pay the modest little fee of which he was then and there relieved. Tutt & Tutt had only two classes of clients: those who paid as they came in, and those who paid as they went out.

Therefore upon hearing Mr. Higgleby's announcement as to the nature of his trouble Tutt registered horror.

"What? What did you say?" he demanded.

"I said," repeated Mr. Higgleby with a shade of annoyance, "'the fact is, I've been arrested for bigamy.' I don't see any reason for making such a touse about it," he added plaintively.

"Who's making a—a—a touse about it?" inquired Tutt, perceiving that he had taken the wrong tack. "I'm not. I was just a little surprised at a man of your genteel appearance—"

"Oh, rot!" expostulated Mr. Higgleby weakly. "You're just like all of 'em! I suppose you were going to say I didn't look like a bigamist—and all that. Well, cut it! Let's start fair. I *am* a bigamist!"

Tutt regarded him with obvious curiosity. "You don't say!" he ejaculated, much as if he wished to add: "How does it feel?"

"I do say!" retorted Mr. Higgleby.

"Well," exclaimed Tutt cheerily, passing into the second phase of the Tutt-Tutt treatment, "after all, bigamy isn't so bad! It's only five years at the worst. Generally it's not more than six months."

"Get wise!" snapped Mr. Higgleby. "I didn't come here to have you throw cold chills into me. I came here to find out how to beat it!"

"Why, certainly! Of course!" protested Tutt hastily.

"I was—"

"And I expect you to get me off!"

"Yes, yes!" murmured Tutt, his usual style completely cramped.

"No matter what!"

"Yes," faintly tuttered Tutt.

"Well," continued Higgleby, taking out a cigar that in shape and looseness of wrapping closely resembled its owner, "now that's settled, let's get down to brass tacks. Here's a copy of the indictment."

He produced a document bearing a large gold seal.

"Those robbers made me pay a dollar-sixty for certification!" he remarked peevishly, indicating the ornament. "What good is certification to me? As if I wanted to pay to make sure I was accused in exact language! Anybody can draw an indictment for bigamy!"

COURT OF GENERAL SESSIONS OF THE PEACE IN AND FOR THE COUNTY OF NEW YORK

The People of the State of New York against
THEOPHILUS HIGGLEBY

The Grand Jury of the County of New York, by this indictment, accuse Theophilus Higgleby of the crime of bigamy, committed as follows:

The said Theophilus Higgleby, late of the borough of Manhattan of the city of New York in the county of New York, aforesaid, on the eleventh day of May in the year of our Lord one thousand nine hundred and nineteen, at Cook County and the city of Chicago in the state of Illinois, did marry one Tomascene Startup, and her, the said Tomascene Startup, did then and there have for his wife;

And afterward, to wit, on the seventeenth day of December in the year of our Lord one thousand nine hundred and nineteen, at the borough of Manhattan of the city of New York in the county of New York aforesaid, did feloniously marry and take as his wife one Alvina Woodcock, and to the said Alvina Woodcock was then and there married, the said Tomascene Startup being then and there living and in full life, against the form of the statute in such case made and provided, and against the peace of the people of the state of New York and their dignity.

JEREMIAH PECKHAM,
District Attorney.

Such was the precise accusation against the isosceles-triangular client, who now sat so limply and disjointedly on the opposite side of Tutt's desk with a certain peculiar air of assurance all his own, as if, though surprised and somewhat annoyed at the grand jury's interference with his private affairs, he was nevertheless—being captain of his own soul—not particularly disturbed about the matter.

"And—er—did you marry these two ladies?" inquired Tutt apologetically.

"Sure!" responded Higgleby without hesitation.

"May I ask why?"

"Why not?" returned Higgleby. "I'm a traveling man."

"Look here," suddenly demanded Tutt. "Were you ever a lawyer?"

"Sure I was!" responded Mr. Higgleby. "I was a member of the bar of Osceola County, Florida."

"You don't say!" gasped Tutt.

"And what, may I ask, are you now?"

"Now I'm a bigamist!" answered Mr. Higgleby.

We forget precisely who it was that so observantly said to another, "Much learning doth make thee mad." At any rate the point to be noted is that overindulgence in erudition has always been known to have an unfortunate effect upon the intellectual faculty. Too much wine—though it must have required an inordinate quantity in certain mendacious periods—was regarded as provocative of truth; and too many books as clearly put bats in a man's belfry. The explanation is of course simple enough. If one overweights the head the whole structure is apt to become unbalanced. This is the reason why we hold scholars in such light esteem. They are an unbalanced lot. And after all, why should they get paid more than half the wage of plumbers or locomotive firemen? What is easier than sitting before a comfortable steam radiator and reading an etymological dictionary or the Laws of Hammurabi? They toil not even if their heads spin. Only in Germany has the pedagogue ever received full meed of gold and of honor—and look at Germany!

Pedants have never been much considered by men of action. They never will be. Experience is the only teacher, which, in the language of Amos Eno, who left two millions to the Institute of Mechanics and Tradesmen, is "worth a damn." We Americans abhor any affectation of learning; hence our weakness for slang. I should apologize for the word "weakness." On the contrary it is a token of our virile independence, our scorn for the delicatessen of education, mere dilettanteism. And this has its practical side, for if we don't know how to pronounce the words "evanescent persiflage" we can call it "bunk" or "rot." We suspect all college graduates. We don't want them in our business. They slink through our lives like pickpockets fearful of detection.

What has all this to do with anything? It has to do, dear reader, with Mr. Caput Magnus, the assistant of the district attorney of the county of New York, whose duty it was to present the evidence in all criminal cases to the grand jury and make ready the instruments of torture known as bills of indictment for that august body's action thereon.

For by all the lights of the Five Points, Chinatown—Mulberry, Canal, Franklin, Lafayette and Centre streets—Pontin's Restaurant, Moe Levy's One Price Tailoring Establishment, and even by those of the glorious days of Howe & Hummel, by the Nine Gods of Law—and more—Caput Magnus was a learned savant. He and he alone of all the members of the bar on the pay roll of the prosecutor's office, housed in their smoke-hung cubicles in the Criminal Courts Building, knew how to draw up those complicated and awful things with their barbed-wire entanglements of "saids," "then and there beings," "with intents," "dids," "to wits," and "aforesaids" in all the verbal chaos with which the law requires those accused of crime to be "simply, clearly and directly" informed of the nature of the offense charged against them, in order that they may know what to do about it and prepare their defense.

And while we are on it—and in order that the reader may be fully instructed and qualified to pursue Tutt & Tutt through their various adventures hereafter— we may as well add that herein lies one of the pitfalls of crime; for the simple-minded burglar or embezzler may blithely make way with a silver service or bundle of bank notes only to find himself floundering, horse, foot and dragoons, in a quagmire of phraseology from which he cannot escape, wriggle as he will. Many such a one has thrown up his hands—and with them silver service, bank notes and all—in horror at what the grand jury has alleged against him.

Indeed there is a well-authenticated tradition that a certain gentleman of color who had inadvertently acquired some poultry belonging to another, when brought to the bar and informed that he theretofore, to wit, in a specified year of our Lord in the night time of the day aforesaid, the outhouse of one Jones then and there situate, feloniously, burglariously did break into and enter with intent to commit a crime therein, to wit, the goods, chattels and personal property of the said Jones then and there being found, then and there feloniously and burglariously by force of arms and against the peace of the people to seize, appropriate and carry away, raised his voice in anguish and cried:

"Fo de Lawd sake, jedge, Ah didn't do none ob dem tings—all Ah done was to take a couple ob chickens!"

Thus to annihilate a man by pad and pencil is indeed an art worthy of admiration. The pen of an indictment clerk is oft mightier than the sword of a Lionheart, the brain behind the subtle quill far defter than said swordsman's skill. Moreover, the ingenuity necessary to draft one of these documents is not confined to its mere successful composition, for having achieved the miraculous feat of alleging in fourteen ways without punctuation that the defendant did something, and with a final fanfare of "saids" and "to wits" inserted his verb where no one will ever find it, the indicter must then be able to unwind himself, rolling in and out among the "dids" and "thens" and "theres" until he is once more safely upon the terra firma of foolscap at the head of the first page.

Mr. Caput Magnus could do it—with the aid of a volume of printed forms devised in the days of Jeremy Bentham. In fact, like a camel who smells water afar off, he could in a desert of verbal sand unerringly find an oasis of meaning. Therefore was Caput Magnus held in high honor among the pack of human hounds who bayed at the call of Huntsman Peckham's horn. Others might lose the scent of what it was all about in the tropical jungle of an indictment eleven pages long, but not he. Like the old dog in Masefield's "Reynard the Fox," Mr. Magnus would work through ditches full of legal slime, nose through thorn thickets of confusion, dash through copses and spinneys of words and phrases, until he snapped close at the heels of intelligibility. The Honorable Peckham couldn't have drawn an indictment to save his legal life. Neither could any of the rest. Neither could Caput without his book of ancient forms—though he didn't let anybody know it.

Shrouded in mystery on a salary of five thousand dollars a year, Caput sat in the shrine of his inner office producing literature of a clarity equaled only by that of George Meredith or Mr. Henry James. He was the Great Accuser. He could call a man a thief in more different ways than any deputy assistant district attorney known to memory—with the aid of his little book. He could lasso and throw any galloping criminal, however fierce, with a gracefully uncoiling rope of deadly adjectives. On all of which he properly prided himself until he became unendurable to his fellows and insufferable to Peckham, who would have cheerfully fired him months gone by had he had a reason or had there been any other legal esoteric to take his place.

Yet pride goeth before a fall. And I am glad of it, for Magnus was a conceited little ass. This yarn is about the fall of Caput Magnus almost as much as it is about the uxorious Higgleby, though the two are inextricably entwined together.

"Mr. Tutt," remarked Tutt after Higgleby's departure, "that new client of ours is certainly *sui generis*."

"That's no crime," smiled the senior partner, reaching for the malt-extract bottle.

"His knowledge of matrimony and the laws governing the domestic relations is certainly exhaustive—not to say exhausting. I look like a piker beside him."

"For which," replied Mr. Tutt, "you may well be thankful."

"I am," replied Tutt devoutly. "But you could put what I know about bigamy in that malt-extract bottle."

"I prefer the present contents!" retorted Mr. Tutt. "Bigamy is a fascinating crime, involving as it does such complicated subjects as the history of the institution of marriage, the ecclesiastical or canonical law governing divorce and annulment, the interesting doctrines of affinity and consanguinity, suits for alienation of affection and criminal conversation, the conflict of laws, the White Slave Act—"

"Interstate commerce, so to speak?" suggested Tutt mischievously.

"Condonation, collusion and connivance," continued Mr. Tutt, brushing him aside, "reinstitution of conjugal rights, the law of feme sole, The Married Woman's Act, separation *a mensa et thoro*, abandonment, jurisdiction, alimony, custody of children, precontract—"

"Help! You're breaking my heart!" cried Tutt. "No little lawyer could know all about such things. It would take a big lawyer."

"Not at all! Not at all!" soothed Mr. Tutt, sipping his eleven-o'clock nourishment and fingering for a stogy. "When it comes to divorce one lawyer knows as much about the law as another. Not even the Supreme Court is able to tell whether a man and woman are really married or not without calling in outside assistance."

"Well, who can?" asked Tutt anxiously.

"Nobody," replied his partner with gravity, biting off the end of a last year's stogy salvaged from the bottom of the letter basket. "Once a man's married his troubles not only begin but never end."

"By the way," said Tutt, "speaking of this sort of thing, I see that that Frenchman whom we referred to our Paris correspondent has just been granted a divorce from his American wife."

"You mean the French diplomat who married the Yankee vaudeville artist in China?"

"Yes," answered Tutt. "You recall they met in Shanghai and took a flying trip to Mongolia, where they were married by a Belgian missionary. The court held that the marriage was invalid, as the French statutes require a native of that country marrying abroad to have the ceremony performed either before a French diplomatic official or 'according to the usages of the country in which the marriage is performed.'"

"Wasn't the Belgian missionary a diplomatic official?" asked Mr. Tutt.

"Evidently not sufficiently so," replied his partner. "Anyhow, in Mongolia there are only two methods sanctified by tradition by which a man may secure a wife—capture or purchase."

"Well, didn't our client capture the actress?"

"Only with her consent—which I assume would be collusion under the French law," said Tutt. "And he certainly didn't buy her—though he might have. It appears that in that happy land a wife costs from five camels up; five camels for a flapper and so on up to thirty or forty camels for an old widow, who invariably brings the highest quotation."

"In Mongolia age evidently ripens and mellows women as it does wine in other countries," reflected Mr. Tutt.

"But you can buy some women for five pounds of rice," added Tutt. "Queer country, isn't it?"

"Not at all!" declared his senior. "Even in America every man pays and pays and pays for his wife—through the nose!"

Tutt grinned appreciatively.

"However that may be," he ventured, "a man who enters into a marriage contract—"

"Marriage isn't a contract," interrupted Mr. Tutt.

"What is it?"

"It's a status—something entirely different—like slavery."

"It's like slavery all right!" agreed Tutt. "But we always speak of a contract of marriage, don't we?"

"Quite inaccurately. The only contract in a marriage is what we commonly refer to as the engagement; that is a real contract and is governed by the laws of contracts. The marriage itself is an entirely different thing. When a marriage is performed and consummated the parties have changed their condition; they bear an entirely new relationship to society, which, as represented by the state, acquires an interest in the transaction, and all you can say about it is that whereas they were both single before, they are married now, and that in the eyes of the law their status has been altered to one as distinct and clearly defined as that which exists between father and son, guardian and ward or master and slave."

"Hear! Hear!" remarked Tutt. "But I don't see why it isn't a contract—or very much like one," he persisted.

"It is like one in that its validity, like that of civil contracts generally, is determined by the law governing the place where it was entered into," went on Mr. Tutt oracularly, as if addressing the court of appeals. "But it differs from a contract for the reason that the parties are not free to fix its terms, which are determined for them by the state; that they cannot modify or rescind it by mutual consent; that the nature of the marriage status changes with the state and the laws of the state where the parties happen to be domiciled; and that damages cannot be recovered for a breach of marital duty."

"Do you know I never thought of that before," admitted Tutt. "But it's perfectly true."

"It is to the interest of society to have the relationship orderly and permanent," continued his partner. "That is why the state is so alert with regard to divorce proceedings and vigilant to prevent fraud or collusion. You may say that the state is always a party to every matrimonial action—even if it is not actually interpleaded—and that such proceedings are triangular and minus many of the characteristics of the ordinary civil suit."

"I suppose another reason for that is that originally marriage and divorce were entirely in the hands of the church, weren't they?" ruminated Tutt.

"Exactly. From very early days in England the church claimed jurisdiction of all matters pertaining to marriage, on the ground that it was a sacrament."

"Did the ecclesiastical courts take the position that all marriages were made in heaven?"

Mr. Tutt shrugged his shoulders.

"'Once married, always married,' was their doctrine."

"Then how did people who were unhappily married get rid of one another?"

"They didn't—if the courts ruled that they had actually been married—but that left a loophole. When was a marriage not a marriage? Answer: When the parties were closely enough related by blood or marriage, or either of them was mentally incapable, under age, victims of duress, fraud, mistake, previously contracted for, or—already married."

"Ah!" breathed Tutt, thinking of Mr. Higgleby.

"The ecclesiastical law remained without any particular variation until after the American Revolution and the colonies separated from Great Britain, and as there was no union of church and state on this side of the water, and so no church to take control of the subject or ecclesiastical courts to put its doctrines into effect, for a while there was no divorce law at all over here, and then one by one the states took the matter up and began to make such laws about it as each saw fit. Hence the jolly old mess we are in now!"

"Jolly for us," commented Tutt. "It means dollars per year to us. Well," he remarked, stretching his legs and yawning, "divorce is sure an evil."

"That's no news," countered Mr. Tutt. "It was just as much of an evil in the time of Moses, of Julius Caesar, and of Edward the Confessor as it is now. There hasn't been anything approaching the flagrancy of Roman divorce in modern history."

"Thank heaven there's still enough to pay our office rent—anyhow!" said Tutt contentedly. "I hope they won't do anything so foolish as to pass a national divorce law."

"They won't," Mr. Tutt assured him. "Most Congressmen are lawyers and are not going to take the bread out of their children's mouths. Besides, the power to regulate the domestic relations of the United States, not being delegated under the Constitution to the Federal Government, is expressly retained by the states themselves."

"You've given me a whole lot of ideas," admitted Tutt. "If I get you rightly, as each state is governed by its own independent laws, the status of married persons must be governed by the law of the state where they are; otherwise if every couple on some theory of exterritoriality carried the law of the state where they happened to have been joined together round with them we would have the spectacle of every state in the union interpreting the divorce laws of every other state—confusion worse confounded."

"On the other hand," returned Mr. Tutt, "the law is settled that a marriage valid when made is valid everywhere; and conversely, if invalid where made is invalid everywhere—like our Mongolian case. If that were not so every couple in order to continue legally married would have to go through a new ceremony in every state through which they traveled."

"Right-o!" whistled Tutt. "A parson on every Pullman!"

"It follows," continued Mr. Tutt, lighting a fresh stogy and warming to his subject, "that as each state has the right to regulate the status of its own citizens it has jurisdiction to act in a divorce proceeding provided one of the parties is actually domiciled within its borders. Naturally this action must be determined by its own laws and not by those of any other state. The great divergence of these laws makes extraordinary complications."

"Hallelujah!" cried Tutt. "Now, in the words of the psalmist, you've said a mouthful! I know a man who at one and the same time is legally married to one woman in England, to another in Nevada, is a bigamist in New York, and—"

"What else could he be except a widower in Pittsburgh?" pondered the elder Tutt. "But it's quite possible. There's a case going on now where a woman in

New York City is suing her ex-husband for a divorce on the usual statutory ground, and naming his present wife as co-respondent, though the plaintiff herself divorced him ten years ago in Reno, and he married again immediately after on the strength of it."

"I'm feeling stronger every minute!" exclaimed Tutt. "Surely in all this bedlam we ought to be able to acquit our new client Mr. Higgleby of the charge of bigamy. At least *you* ought to be able to. I couldn't."

"What's the difficulty?" queried Mr. Tutt.

"The difficulty simply is that he married the present Mrs. Higgleby on the seventeenth of last December here in the city of New York, when he had a perfectly good wife, whom he had married on the eleventh of the preceding May, living in Chicago."

"What on earth is the matter with him?" inquired Mr. Tutt.

"He simply says he's a traveling man," replied his partner, "and—he happened to be in New York."

"Well, the next time he calls, you send him in to see me," directed Mr. Tutt. "What was the present lady's name?"

"Woodcock," answered Tutt. "Alvina Woodcock."

"And she wanted to change to Higgleby?" muttered his partner. "I wonder why."

"Oh, there's something sort of appealing about him," acknowledged Tutt. "But he don't look like a bigamist," he concluded. "What does a bigamist look like?" meditated Mr. Tutt as he lit another stogy.

"Good morning, Mr. Tutt," muttered the Honorable Peckham from behind the imitation rubber plant in his office, where he was engaged in surreptitiously consuming an apple. "Um—be with you in a minute. What's on your mind?"

Mr. Tutt simultaneously removed his stogy with one hand and his stovepipe with the other.

"I thought we might as well run over my list of cases," he replied. "I can offer you a plea or two if you wish."

"Do I!" ejaculated the D.A., rolling his eyes heavenward. "Let's hear the Roll of Honor."

Mr. Tutt placed his hat, bottom side up, on the carpet and lowered himself into a huge leather armchair, furnished to the county by a political friend of Mr. Peckham and billed at four hundred per cent of the regular retail price. Then he reinserted the stogy between his lips and produced from his inside pocket a typewritten sheet.

"There's Watkins—murdered his stepmother—indicted seven months ago. Give you murder in the second?"

"I'll take it," assented Peckham, lighting a cigar in a businesslike manner. "What else you got?"

"Joseph Goldstein—burglary. Will you give him grand larceny in the second?" The Honorable Peckham shook his head.

"Sorry I can't oblige you, old top," he said regretfully. "He's called the King of the Fences. If I did, the papers would holler like hell. I'll make it any degree of burglary, though."

"Very well. Burglary in the third," agreed Mr. Tutt, jotting it down. "Then here's a whole bunch—five—indicted together for assault on a bartender."

"What degree?"

"Second—brass knuckles."

"You can have third degree for the lot," grunted Peckham laconically.

"All right," said Mr. Tutt. "Now for the ones that are going to trial. Here's Jennie Smith, indicted for stealing a mandarin chain valued at sixty-five dollars up at Monahaka's. The chain's only worth about six-fifty and I can prove it. Monahaka don't want to go to trial because he knows I'll show him up for the Oriental flimflammer that he is. But of course she took it. What do you say? I'll plead her to petty and you give her a suspended sentence? That's a fair trade."

Peckham pondered.

"Sure," he said finally. "I'm agreeable. Only tell Jennie that next time I'll have her run out of town."

Mr. Tutt nodded.

"I'll whisper it to her. Now then, here's Higgleby—"

"Higgle who?" inquired Peckham dreamily.

"Bee—by—Higgleby," explained Mr. Tutt. "For bigamy. I want you to dismiss the indictment for me."

"What for?"

"You'll never convict him."

"Why not?"

"Just because you never will!" Mr. Tutt assured him with earnestness. "And you might as well wipe him off the list."

"Anything the matter with the indictment?" asked the D.A. "Caput Magnus drew it. He's a good man, you know."

Mr. Tutt drew sententiously on his stogy.

"I would like to tell you all my secrets," he replied after a pause, "but I can't afford to. The indictment is in the usual form. But just between you and me, you'll never convict Higgleby as long as you live."

"Didn't he marry two joint and several ladies?"

"He did."

"And one of 'em right here in New York County?"

"He did."

"Well, how in hell can I dismiss the indictment?"

"Oh, easily enough. Lack of proof as to the first marriage in Chicago, for instance. How are you going to prove he wasn't divorced?"

"That's matter of defense," retorted Peckham.

"What's a little bigamy between friends, anyway?" ruminated the old lawyer. "It's a kind of sumptuary offense. People will marry. And it's good policy to have 'em. If they happen to overdo it a little—"

"Well, if I do chuck the darn thing out what will you give me in return?" asked Peckham. "Of course, bigamy isn't my favorite crime or anything like that. I'm no bloodhound on matrimonial offenses. How'll you trade?"

"If you'll throw out Higgleby I'll plead Angelo Ferrero to manslaughter," announced Mr. Tutt with a grand air of bestowing largess upon an unworthy recipient.

"Cock-a-doodle-do!" chortled Peckham. "A lot you will! Angelo's halfway to the chair already yet!"

"That's the best I'll do," replied Mr. Tutt, feeling for his hat.

Peckham hesitated. Mr. Tutt was a fair dealer. And he wanted to get rid of Angelo.

"Give you murder in the second," he urged.

"Manslaughter."

"Nothing doing," answered the D.A. definitely. "Your Mr. Higglebigamy'll have to stand trial."

"Oh, very well!" replied Mr. Tutt, unjointing himself. "We're ready—whenever you are."

The old lawyer's lank figure had hardly disappeared out of the front office when Peckham rang for Caput Magnus.

"Look here, Caput," he remarked suspiciously to the indictment clerk, "is there anything wrong with that Higgledy indictment?"

"Higgleby, you mean, I guess," replied Mr. Magnus, regarding the D.A. in a superior manner over the tops of his horn-rimmed spectacles. "Nothing is the matter with the indictment. I have followed my customary form. It has stood every test over and over again. Why do you ask?"

The Honorable Peckham turned away impatiently.

"Oh—nothing. Look here," he added unexpectedly, "I think I'll have you try that indictment yourself."

"Me!" ejaculated Caput in horror. "Why, I never tried a case in my life!"

"Well, 's time you began!" growled the D.A.

"I—I—shouldn't know what to do!" protested Mr. Magnus in agony at the mere suggestion.

"Where the devil would we be if everybody felt like that?" demanded his master. "You're supposed to be a lawyer, aren't you?"

"But I—I—can't! I—don't know how!"

"Hang it all," cried Peckham furiously, "you go ahead and do as I say. You indicted Higgledy; now you can try Higgledy!"

He was utterly unreasonable, but his anger was genuine if baseless.

"Oh, very well, sir," stammered Mr. Magnus. "Of course I'll—I must—do whatever you say."

"You better!" shouted Peckham after his retreating figure. "You little blathering shrimp!"

Then he threw himself down in his swivel chair with a bang.

"Judas H. Priest!" he roared at the rubber plant. "I'd give a good deal for a decent excuse to fire that blooming nincompoop!"

Meantime, as the object of his ire slunk down the corridor darkness descended upon the soul of Caput Magnus. For Caput was what is known as an office lawyer and had never gone into court save as an onlooker or—as he would have phrased it—an *amicus curiae*. He was a perfect pundit—"a hellion on law," according to the Honorable Peckham—a strutting little cock on his own particular dunghill, but, stripped of his goggles, books, forms and foolscap, as far as his equanimity was concerned he might as well have been in face, figure and general objectionability. No longer could he be heard roaring for his stenographer. Instead, those of his colleagues who paused stealthily outside his door on their way over to Pont's for "five-o'clock tea" heard dulcet tones floating forth from the transom in varying fluctuations:

"Ahem! H'm! Gentlemen of the jury—h'm! The defendant is indicted for the outrageous crime of bigamy! No, that won't do! Gentlemen of the jury, the defendant is indicted for the crime of bigamy! H'm! The crime of bigamy is one of those atrocious offenses against the moral law—"

"Oh! Oh!" choked the legal assistants as they embraced themselves wildly. "Oh! Oh! Caput's practisin'! Just listen to 'im! Ain't he the little cuckoo! Bet he's takin' lessons in elocution! But won't old Tutt just eat him alive!"

And in the stilly hours of the early dawn those sleeping in tenements and extensions adjacent to the hall bedroom occupied by Caput were roused by a trembling voice that sought vainly to imitate the nonchalance of experience, declaiming: "Gentlemen of the jury, the defendant is indicted for the crime of bigamy! This offense is one repugnant to the instincts of civilization and odious to the tenets of religion!" And thereafter they tossed until breakfast time, bigamy becoming more and more odious to them every minute.

No form of diet, no physical exercise, no "reducicle" could have achieved the extraordinary alteration in Mr. Magnus' appearance that was in fact induced by his anxiety over his prospective prosecution of Higgleby. Whereas erstwhile he had been smug and condescending, complacent, lethargic and ponderous, he now became drawn, nervous, apprehensive and obsequious. Moreover, he was markedly thinner. He was obviously on a decline, caused by sheer funk. Speak sharply to him and he would shy like a frightened pony. The Honorable Peckham was enraptured, claiming now to have a system of getting even with people that beat the invention of Torquemada. When it was represented to him that Caput might die, fade away entirely, in which case the office would be left without any indictment clerk, the Honorable Peckham profanely declared that he didn't care a damn. Caput Magnus was going to try Higgleby, that was all there was to it! And at last the day came.

Gathered in Judge Russell's courtroom were as many of the office assistants as could escape from their duties, anxious to officiate at the legal demise of Caput Magnus. Even the Honorable Peckham could not refrain from having business there at the call of the calendar. It resembled a regular monthly conference of the D.A.'s professional staff, which for some reason Tutt and Mr. Tutt had also been invited to attend. Yea, the spectators were all there in the legal colosseum waiting eagerly to see Caput Magnus enter the arena to be gobbled up by Tutt & Tutt. They thirsted for his blood, having been for years bored by his brains.

They would rather see Caput Magnus made mincemeat of than ninety-nine criminals convicted, even were they guilty of bigamy.

But as yet Caput Magnus was not there. It was ten-twenty-nine. The clerk was there; Mr. Higgleby, isosceles, flabby and acephalous as ever, was there; Tutt and Mr. Tutt were there; and Bonnie Doon, and the stenographer and the jury. And on the front bench the two wives of Higgleby sat, side by side, so frigidly that had that gentleman possessed the gift of prevision he would never have married either of them; Mrs. Tomascene Startup Higgleby and Mrs.—or Miss—Alvina Woodcock (Higgleby)—depending upon the action of the jury. The entire cast in the eternal matrimonial triangular drama was there except the judge and the prosecutor in the form of Caput Magnus.

And then, preceding the judge by half a minute only, his entrance timed histrionically to the second, he came, like Eudoxia, like a flame out of the east. In swept Caput Magnus with all the dignity and grace of an Irving playing Cardinal Wolsey. Haggard, yes; pale, yes; tremulous, perhaps; but nevertheless glorious in a new cutaway coat, patent-leather shoes, green tie, a rosebud blushing from his lapel, his hair newly cut and laid down in beautiful little wavelets with pomatum, his figure erect, his chin in air, a book beneath his arm, his right hand waving in a delicate gesture of greeting; for Caput had taken O'Leary's suggestion seriously, and had purchased that widely known and authoritative work to which so many eminent barristers owe their entire success—"How to Try a Case"—and in it he had learned that in order to win the hearts of the jury one should make oneself beautiful.

"What in hell's he done to himself?" gasped O'Leary to O'Brien.

"He'll make a wonderful corpse!" whispered the latter in response.

"Order in the court! His Honor the Judge of General Sessions!" bellowed an officer at this moment, and the judge came in.

Everybody got up. He bowed. Everybody bowed. Everybody sat down again. A few, deeply affected, blew their noses. Then His Honor smiled genially and asked what business there was before the court, and the clerk told him that they were all there to try a man named Higgleby for bigamy, and the judge, nodding at Caput, said to go ahead and try him.

In the bottom of his peritoneum Mr. Magnus felt that he carried a cold stone the size of a grapefruit. His hands were ice, his lips bloodless. And there was a Niagara where his hearing should have been. But he rose, just as the book told him to do, in all his beauty, and enunciated in the crystal tones he had learned during the last few weeks at Madam Winterbottom's school of acting and elocution—in syllables chiseled from the stone of eloquence by the lapidary of culture:

"If Your Honor please, I move the cause of the People of the state of New York against Theophilus Higgleby, indicted for bigamy."

Peckham and the rest couldn't believe their ears. It wasn't possible! That perfect specimen of tonsorial and sartorial art, warbling like a legal Caruso, conducting himself so naturally, easily and casually, couldn't be old Caput Magnus! They pinched themselves.

"Say!" ejaculated Peckham. "What's happened to him? When did Sir Henry sign up with us?"

Mr. Tutt across the inclosure in front of the jury box raised his bushy eyebrows and looked whimsically at the D. A. over his spectacles.

"Are you ready, Mr. Tutt?" inquired the judge.

"Entirely so, Your Honor," responded the lawyer.

"Then impanel a jury."

The jury was impaneled, Mr. Caput Magnus passing through that trying ordeal with great éclat.

"You may proceed to open your case," directed the judge.

The staff saw a very white Caput Magnus rise and bow in the direction of the bench. Then he stepped to the jury box and cleared his throat. His official associates held their breath expectantly. Would he—or wouldn't he? There was a pause.

Then: "Mister Foreman and gentlemen of the jury," declaimed Caput in flutelike tones: "The defendant is indicted for the crime of bigamy, an offense alike repugnant to religion, civilization and to the law."

The words flowed from him like a rippling sunlit stream; encircled him like a necklace of verbal jewels, a rosary, each word a pearl or a bead or whatever it is. With perfect articulation, enunciation and gesticulation Mr. Caput Magnus went on to inform his hearers that Mr. Higgleby was a bigamist of the deepest dye, that he had feloniously, wilfully and knowingly married two several females, and by every standard of conduct was utterly and entirely detestable.

Mr. Higgleby, flanked by Tutt and Mr. Tutt, listened calmly. Caput warmed to his task.

The said Higgleby, said he, had as aforesaid in the indictment committed the act of bigamy, to wit, of marriage when he had one legal wife already, in New York City on the seventeenth of last December, by marrying in Grace Church Chantry the lady whom they saw sitting by the other lady—he meant the one with the red feather in her bonnet—that is to say, her hat, whereas the other lady, as he had said aforesaid, had been lawfully and properly married to the defendant the preceding May, to wit, in Chicago as aforesaid—

"Pardon me!" interrupted the foreman petulantly. "Which is the lady you mean was married to the defendant in New York? You said she was sitting by the other lady and that you meant the one with the red feather, but you didn't say whether the one with the red feather was the other lady or the one you were talking about."

Caput gagged and turned pink.

"I—I—" he stammered. "The lady in the red bonnet is—the—New York lady."

"You mean she isn't his wife although the defendant went through the form of marriage with her, because he was already married to another," suggested His Honor. "You might, I think, put things a little more simply. However, do it your own way."

"Ye-es, Your Honor."

"Go on."

But Caput was lost—hopelessly. Every vestige of the composure so laboriously acquired at Madam Winterbottom's salon had evaporated. He felt as if he were swinging in midair hitched to a scudding aeroplane by a rope about his middle. The mucous membranes of his throat were as dry and as full of dust as the entrails of a carpet sweeper. His vision was blurred and he had no control over his muscles. Weakly he leaned against the table in front of the jury, the room swaying about him. The pains of hell gat hold upon him. He was dying. Even the staff felt compunction—all but the Honorable Peckham.

Judge Russell quickly sensed the situation. He was a kindly man, who had pulled many an ass out of the mire of confusion. So with a glance at Mr. Tutt he came to Caput's rescue.

"Let us see, Mr. Magnus," he remarked pleasantly; "suppose you prove the Illinois marriage first. Is Mrs. Higgleby in court?"

Both ladies started from their seats.

"Mrs. Tomascene Higgleby," corrected His Honor. "Step this way, please, madam!"

The former Miss Startup made her way diffidently to the witness chair and in a faint voice answered the questions relative to her marriage of the preceding spring as put to her by the judge. Mr. Tutt waved her aside and Caput Magnus felt returning strength. He had expected and prepared for a highly technical assault upon the legality of the ceremony performed in Cook County. He had anticipated every variety and form of question. But Mr. Tutt put none. He merely smiled benignly upon Caput in an avuncular fashion.

"Have you no questions, Mr. Tutt?" inquired His Honor.

"None," answered the lawyer.

"Then prove the bigamous marriage," directed Judge Russell.

Then rose at the call of justice, militantly and with a curious air of proprietorship in the overmarried defendant, the wife or maiden who in earlier days had answered to the name of Alvina Woodcock. Though she was the injured party and though the blame for her unfortunate state rested entirely upon Higgleby, her resentment seemed less directed toward the offending male than toward the Chicago lady who was his lawful wife. There was no question as to the circumstances to which she so definitely and aggressively testified. No one could gainsay the deplorable fact that she had, as she supposed, been linked in lawful wedlock to Mr. Tutt's isosceles client. But there was that in her manner which suggested that she felt that being the last she should be first, that finding was keeping, and that possession was nine points of matrimonial law.

And, as before, Mr. Tutt said nothing. Neither he nor Tutt nor Bonnie Doon nor yet Higgleby showed any the least sign of concern. Caput's momentarily returning self-possession forsook him. What portended his ominous silence? Had he made some horrible mistake? Had he overlooked some important jurisdictional fact? Was he now to be hoist for some unknown reason by his own petard? He was, poor innocent—he was!

"That is the case," he announced faintly. "The People rest."

Judge Russell looked down curiously at Mr. Tutt.

"Well," he remarked, "how about it, Mr. Tutt?"

But the old lawyer only smiled.

"Come here a minute," directed His Honor.

And when Mr. Tutt reached the bench the judge said: "Have you any defense in this case? If not, why don't you plead guilty and let me dispose of the matter?"

"But, Your Honor," protested Mr. Tutt, "of course I have a defense—and a most excellent one!"

"You have?"

"Certainly."

The judged elevated his forehead.

"Very well," he remarked; "if you really have one you had better go on with it. And," he added beneath his breath, but in a tone clearly audible to the clerk, "the Lord have mercy on your soul!"

The assistants saw Caput subside into his chair and simultaneously Mr. Tutt slowly raise his lank form toward the ceiling.

"Gentlemen of the jury," said he benignly: "My client, Mr. Higgleby, is charged in this indictment with the crime of bigamy committed here in New York, in marrying Alvina Woodcock—the strong-minded lady on the front row of benches there—when he already had a lawful wife living in Chicago. The indictment alleges no other offense and the district attorney has not sought to prove any, my learned and eloquent adversary, Mr. Magnus, having a proper regard for the constitutional rights of every unfortunate whom he brings to the bar of justice. If therefore I can prove to you that Mr. Higgleby was never lawfully married to Tomascene Startup in Chicago on the eleventh of last May or at any other time, the allegation of bigamy falls to the ground; at any rate so far as this indictment is concerned. For unless the indictment sets forth a valid prior marriage it is obvious that the subsequent marriage cannot be bigamous. Am I clear? I perceive by your very intelligent facial expressions that I am. Well, my friends, Mr. Higgleby never was lawfully married to Tomascene Startup last May in Chicago, and you will therefore be obliged to acquit him! Come here, Mr. Smithers."

Caput Magnus suddenly experienced the throes of dissolution. Who was Smithers? What could old Tutt be driving at? But Smithers—evidently the Reverend Sanctimonious Smithers—was already placidly seated in the witness chair, his limp hands folded across his stomach and his thin nose looking interrogatively toward Mr. Tutt.

"What is your name?" asked the lawyer dramatically.

"My name is Oswald Garrison Smithers," replied the reverend gentleman in Canton-flannel accents, "and I reside in Pantuck, Iowa, where I am pastor of the Reformed Lutheran Church."

"Do you know the defendant?"

"Indeed I do," sighed the Reverend Smithers. "I remember him very well. I solemnized his marriage to a widow of my congregation on July 4, 1917; in fact to the relict of our late senior warden, Deacon Pellatiah Higgins. Sarah Maria Higgins was the lady's name, and she is alive and well at the present time."

He gazed deprecatingly at the jury. If meekness had efficacy he would have inherited the earth.

"What?" ejaculated the foreman. "You say this man is married to *three* women?"

"Trigamy—not bigamy!" muttered the clerk, *sotto voce*.

"You have put your finger upon the precise point, Mister Foreman!" exclaimed Mr. Tutt admiringly. "If Mr. Higgleby was already lawfully married to a lady in Iowa when he married Miss—or Mrs.—Startup in Chicago last May, his marriage to the latter was not a legal marriage; it was in fact no marriage at all. You can't charge a man with bigamy unless you recite a legal marriage followed by an illegal one. Therefore, since the indictment fails to set forth a legal marriage anywhere followed by a marriage, legal or otherwise, in New York County, it recites no crime, and my client must be acquitted. Is not that the law, Your Honor?"

Judge Russell quickly hid a smile and turned to the moribund Caput.

"Mr. Magnus, have you anything to say in reply to Mr. Tutt's argument?" he asked. "If not—"

But no response came from Caput Magnus. He was past all hearing, understanding or answering. He was ready to be carried out and buried.

"Well, all I have got to say is—" began the foreman disgustedly.

"You do not have to say anything!" admonished the judge severely. "I will do whatever talking is necessary. A little more care in the preparation of the indictment might have rendered this rather absurd situation impossible. As it is, I must direct an acquittal. The defendant is discharged upon this indictment. But I will hold him in bail for the action of another grand jury."

"In which event we shall have another equally good defense, Your Honor," Mr. Tutt assured him.

"I don't doubt it, Mr. Tutt," returned the judge good-naturedly. "Your client seems to have loved not wisely but too well." And they all poured out happily into the corridor—that is, all of them except Caput and the two ladies, who remained seated upon their bench gazing fiercely and disdainfully at each other like two tabby cats on a fence.

"So you're not married to him, either!" sneered Miss Woodcock.

"Well, I'm as much married to him as you are!" retorted Miss Startup with her nose in the air.

Then instinctively they both turned and with one accord looked malevolently at Caput, who, seeing in their glance something which he did not like, slipped stealthily from his chair and out of the room, leaving ignominiously behind him upon the floor his precious volume entitled "How to Try a Case"!

"That Sort of Woman"

"Judge not according to the appearance."—John VII: 24.

"Tutt," said Mr. Tutt, entering the offices of Tutt & Tutt and hanging his antediluvian stovepipe on the hat-tree in the corner, "I see by the morning paper that Payson Clifford has departed this life."

"You don't say!" replied the junior Tutt, glancing up from the letter he was writing. "Which one,—Payson, Senior, or Payson, Junior?"

"Payson, Senior," answered Mr. Tutt as he snipped off the end of a stogy with the pair of nail scissors which he always carried in his vest pocket.

"In that case, it's too bad," remarked Tutt regretfully.

"Why 'in that case'?" queried his partner.

"Oh, the son isn't so much of a much!" replied the smaller Tutt. "I don't say the father was so much of a much, either. Payson Clifford was a good fellow—even if he wasn't our First Citizen—or likely to be a candidate for that position in the Hereafter. But that boy—"

"Shh!" reproved Mr. Tutt, slowly shaking his head so that the smoke from his rat-tailed cigar wove a gray scroll in the air before his face. "Remember that there's one thing worse than to speak ill of the dead, and that's to speak ill of a client!"

Mr. Payson Clifford, the client in question, was a commonplace young man who had been carefully prepared for the changes and chances of this mortal life first at a Fifth Avenue day school in New York City, afterwards at a select boarding school among the rock-ribbed hills of the Granite State, and finally at Cambridge, Massachusetts, in the cultured atmosphere of Harvard College, through whose precincts, in the dim, almost forgotten past, we are urged to believe that the good and the great trod musingly in their beautiful prime. He emerged with a perhaps almost prudish distaste for the ugly, the vulgar, and the unclean,—and with distinct delusions of grandeur. He was still in that state not badly described by the old saw—"You can always tell a Harvard man,—but you can't tell him much."

His mother had died when he was still a child and he preserved her memory as the most sacred treasure of his inner shrine. He could just recall her as a gentle and dignified presence, in contrast with whom his burly, loud-voiced father had always seemed crass and ordinary. And although it was that same father who had, for as long as he could remember, supplied him with a substantial check upon the first day of every month and thus enabled him to achieve that exalted state of intellectual and spiritual superiority which he had in fact attained, nevertheless, putting it frankly in the vernacular, Payson rather looked down on the old man, who palpably suffered from lack of the advantages which he had furnished to his son.

Payson, Sr., had never taken any particular pains to alter his son's opinion of himself. On the whole he was more proud of him than otherwise, recognizing that while he obviously suffered from an overdevelopment of the ego and an excessive fastidiousness in dress, he was, at bottom, clearly all right and a good sort. Still, he was forced to confess that there wasn't much between them. His son expressed the same thought by regretting that his father "did not speak his language."

So, in the winter vacation when Payson, Sr., fagged from his long day at the office sought the "Frolics" or the "Folies," Payson, Jr., might be seen at a concert for the harpsichord and viola, or at an evening of Palestrina or the Earlier Gregorian Chants. Had he been less supercilious about it this story would never have been written—and doubtless no great loss at that. But it is the prerogative of youth to be arrogantly merciless in its judgment of the old. Its bright lexicon has no verdict "with mitigating circumstances." Youth is just when it is right; it is cruel when it is wrong; and it is inexorable in any case. If we are ever to be tried for our crimes let us have juries of white whiskered old boys who like tobacco, crab flakes, light wines and musical comedy.

All of which leads up to the sad admission upon our part that Payson, Jr., was a prig. And in the very middle of his son's priggishness Payson, Sr., up and died, and Tutt and Mr. Tutt were called upon to administer his estate.

There may be concealed somewhere a few rare human beings who can look back upon their treatment of their parents with honest satisfaction. I have never met any. It is the fate of those who bring others into the world to be chided for their manners, abused for their mistakes, and pilloried for their faults. Twenty years difference in age turns many an elegance into a barbarism; many a virtue into a vice-versa. I do not perform at breakfast for the edification of my offspring upon the mustache cup, but I chew my strawberry seeds, which they claim is worse. My grandpapa and grandmama used to pour the coffee from their cups and drink it from their saucers and they were—nevertheless—rated AA1 in Boston's Back Bay Blue Book. And now my daughters, who smoke cigarettes, object loudly to my pipe smoke! *Autre temps autres manières.* And no man is a hero to his children. He has a hanged-sight more chance with his valet—if in these days he can afford to keep one.

His father's death was a shock to Payson, Jr., because he had not supposed that people in active business like that ever did die,—they "retired" instead, and after a discreet period of semi-seclusion gradually disintegrated by appropriate stages. But Payson, Sr., simply died right in the middle of everything—without any chance of a spiritual understanding—"reconciliation" would be inaccurate—with his son. So, Payson, Jr., protestingly acquired by part cash and balance credit a complete suit of what he scathingly described as "the barbarous panoply of death" and, turning himself into what he similarly called a "human catafalque," followed Payson, Sr., to the grave.

Perhaps, after all, we have been a bit hard on Payson, Jr. He was fundamentally, as his father had perceived, good stuff, and wanted to do the right thing. But what is the right thing? Really it isn't half as hard to be good as to know how.

As the orphaned Payson, ensconced in lonely state in one of the funeral hacks, was carried at a fast trot down Broadway towards the offices of Tutt & Tutt, he consoled himself for his loss with the reflection that this was, probably, the last time he would ever have to see any of his relatives. Never in his short life had he been face to face with such a gathering of unattractive human beings. He hadn't imagined that such people existed. They oughtn't to exist. The earth should be a lovely place, its real estate occupied only by cultured and lovely people. These aesthetic considerations reminded him with a shock that, just as he had been an utter stranger to them, so he had been a stranger to his father—his poor, old, widowed father. What did he really know about him?—not one thing! And he had never tried to find out anything about him,—about his friends, his thoughts, his manner of life,—content merely to cash his checks, under the unconscious assumption that the man who drew them ought to be equally content to be the father of such a youth as himself. But those rusty relatives! They must have been his father's! Certainly his mother's wouldn't have been like that,—and he felt confident he took after his mother. Still, those relatives worried him! Up at Harvard he had stood rather grandly on his name—"Payson Clifford, Jr.,"—with no questions asked about the "Senior" or anybody else. He now perceived that he was to be thrown out into the world of fact where who and what his father had been might make a lot of difference. Rather anxiously he hoped the old gentleman would turn out to have been all right;—and would have left enough of an estate so that he could still go on cashing checks upon the first day of every month!

It was one of the unwritten laws of the office of Tutt & Tutt that Mr. Tutt was never to be bothered about the details of a probate matter, and it is more than doubtful whether, even if he had tried, he could have correctly made out the inventory of an estate for filing in the Surrogate's Court. For be it known that, while the senior member of the firm was long on the philosophy of the law and the subtleties of "restraints on alienation," "powers," "perpetuities" and the mysteries of "the next eventual estate," he was frankly short on the patience to add and subtract. So while Mr. Tutt drew their clients' wills, it was Tutt who attempted to probate and execute them. Then, if by any chance, there was any trouble or some ungrateful relative thought he hadn't got enough, it was Mr. Tutt who reluctantly tossed away his stogy, strolled over to court and defended the will which he had drawn,—usually with success.

So it was the lesser Tutt who wrung the hand of Payson Clifford and gave him the leathern armchair by the window.

"And now about the will!" chirped Tutt, as after a labored encomium upon the virtues of Payson, Senior, deceased, he took the liberty of lighting a cigarette before he commenced to read the instrument which lay in a brown envelope upon the desk before him. "And now about the will! I suppose you are already aware that your father has made you his executor and, after a few minor legacies, the residuary legatee of his entire estate?"

Payson shook his head mutely. He felt it more becoming to pretend to be ignorant of these things under the circumstances.

"Yes," continued Tutt cheerfully, taking up the envelope, "Mr. Tutt drew the will—nearly fifteen years ago—and your father never thought necessary to change it. It's lain right there in our 'Will Box' without being disturbed more than once,—and that was seven or eight years ago when he came in one day and asked to be allowed to look at it,—I think he put an envelope containing a letter in with it. I found one there the other day."

Payson languidly took the will in his hand.

"How large an estate did he leave?" he inquired.

"As near as I can figure out about seventy thousand dollars," answered Tutt. "But the transfer tax will not be heavy, and the legacies do not aggregate more than ten thousand."

The instrument was a short one,—drawn with all Mr. Tutt's ability for compression—and filling only a single sheet. Payson's father had bequeathed seventy-six hundred dollars to his three cousins and their children, and everything else he had left to his son. Payson rapidly computed that after settling the bills against the estate, including that of Tutt & Tutt, he would probably get at least sixty thousand out of it. At the current rate he would continue to be quite comfortable,—more so in fact than heretofore. Still, it was less than he had expected. Perhaps his father had had expensive habits.

"Here's the letter," went on Tutt, handing it to Payson who took out his penknife to open it the more neatly. "Probably a suggestion as to the disposal of personal effects—remembrances or something of the sort. It's often done."

The envelope was a cheap one, ornamented in the upper left hand corner with a wood cut showing a stout goddess in a night dress, evidently meant for Proserpina—pouring a Niagara of grain out of a cornucopia of plenty over a farmland stacked high with apples, corn, and pumpkins, and flooded by the beams of a rising sun with a real face. Beneath were the words:

"If not delivered in five days return to
Clifford, Cobb & Weng,
Grain Dealers and Produce
597 Water Street,
N.Y. City,
N.Y."

Even as his eye fell upon it Payson was conscious of its coarse vulgarity. And "Weng"! Whoever heard of such a name? He certainly had not,—hadn't even known that his father had a partner with such an absurd cognomen! "—& Weng!" There was something terribly plebeian about it. As well as about the obvious desire for symmetry which had led to the addition of that superfluous "N.Y." below the entirely adequate "N.Y. City." But, of course, he'd be glad to do anything his father requested in a letter.

He forced the edge of the blade through the tough fiber of the envelope, drew forth the enclosed sheet and unfolded it. In the middle of the top was a replica of the wood cut upon the outside, only minus the "If not delivered in five days return to." Then Payson read in his father's customary bold scrawl the simple inscription, doomed to haunt him sleeping and waking for many moons:—

"In case of my sudden death I wish my executor to give twenty-five thousand dollars to my very dear friend Sadie Burch, of Hoboken, N.J.

"PAYSON CLIFFORD."

For a brief—very brief—moment, a mist gathered over the letter in the son's hand. "My dear friend Sadie Burch!" He choked back the exclamation of surprise that rose unconsciously to his lips and endeavored to suppress any facial evidence of his inner feelings. "Twenty-five thousand!" Then he held out the letter more or less casually to Tutt.

"Wee-e-ll!" whistled the lawyer softly, with a quick glance from under his eyebrows.

"Oh, it isn't the money!" remarked Payson in a sickly tone—although of course he was lying. It *was* the money.

By Advice of Counsel

The idea of surrendering nearly half his father's estate to a stranger staggered him; yet to his eternal credit, in that first instant of bewildered agony no thought of disregarding his father's wishes entered his mind. It was a hard wallop, but he'd got to stand it.

"Oh, that's nothing!" remarked Tutt. "It's not binding. You don't need to pay any attention to it."

"Do you really mean that that paper hasn't any legal effect?" exclaimed the boy with such a reaction of relief that for the moment the ethical aspect of the case was entirely obscured by the legal.

"None whatever!" returned Tutt definitely.

"But it's part of the will!" protested Payson. "It's in my father's own handwriting."

"That doesn't make any difference," declared the lawyer. "Not being witnessed in the manner required by law it's not of the slightest significance."

"Not even if it is put right in with the will?"

"Not a particle."

"But I've often heard of letters being put with wills."

"No doubt. But I'll wager you never heard of any one of them being probated."

Payson's legal experience in fact did not reach to this technical point.

"Look here!" he returned obstinately. "I'll be hanged if I understand. You say this paper has no legal value and yet it is in my father's own hand and practically attached to his will. Now, apart from any—er—moral question involved, just why isn't this letter binding on me?"

Tutt smiled leniently.

"Have a cigarette?" he asked, and when Payson took one, he added sympathetically as he held a match for him, "Your attitude, my dear sir, does you credit. It is wholly right and natural that you should instinctively desire to uphold that which on its face appears to be a wish of your father. But all the same that letter isn't worth the paper it's written on—as matter of law."

"But why not?" demanded Payson. "What better evidence could the courts desire of the wishes of a testator than such a letter?"

"The reason is simple enough!" replied Tutt, settling himself in a comfortable position. "In the eye of the law no property is ever without an owner. It is always owned by somebody, although the ownership may be in dispute. When a man dies his real property instantly passes to his heirs and his personal property descends in accordance to the local statute of distributions or, if there isn't any, to his next of kin; but if he leaves a will, to the extent to which it is valid, it diverts the property from its natural legal destination. Thus, in effect, the real purpose of a will is to prevent the laws operating on one's estate after death. If your father had died intestate, you would have instantly become, in contemplation of law, the owner of all his property. His will—his legal will—deprives you of a small part of it for the benefit of others. But the law is exceedingly careful about recognizing such an intention of a testator to prevent the operation of the statutes and requires him to demonstrate the sincerity and fixity of that intention by going through various established formalities, such as putting his intention in due form in a written instrument which he must sign and

84

declare to be his last will before a certain number of competent witnesses whom he requests to sign as such and who actually do sign as such in his presence and in the presence of each other. Your father obviously did none of these things when he placed this letter with his will."

"But isn't a letter ever enough—under any circumstances?" inquired Payson.

"Well," said Tutt. "It is true that under certain exceptional circumstances a man may make what is known as a nuncupative will."

"What is a—a—nuncupative will?" asked his client.

"Technically it is an oral will, operating on personality only, made in extremis—that is, actually in fear of death—and under our statutes limited to soldiers in active military service or to mariners at sea. Under the old common law it was just as effective to pass personal estate as a written instrument."

"But father wasn't either a soldier or a sailor," commented Payson, "and anyhow a letter isn't an oral will; if it's anything at all, it's a written one, isn't it?"

"That is the attitude the law takes," nodded Tutt. "Of course, one could argue that it made no difference whether a man uttered his wishes orally in the presence of witnesses or reduced them to writing and signed them, but the law is very technical in such matters and it has been held that a will reduced to writing and signed by the testator, or a memorandum of instructions for making a will, cannot be treated as a nuncupative will; nor is a written will, drawn up by an attorney, but not signed, owing to the sickness of the testator to be treated as a nuncupative will; but upon requisite proof—in a proper case—a paper, not perfected as a written will, may be established as a nuncupative will when its completion is prevented by act of God, or any other cause than an intention to abandon or postpone its consummation. The presumption of the law is against validity of a testamentary paper not completed. There must be in the testator the *animus testandi*, which is sometimes presumed from circumstances in such cases and in such places as nuncupative wills are recognized. Now, your father being as you point out, neither a soldier nor a sailor, couldn't have made a nuncupative will under any circumstances, even if a letter would legally be treated as such a will instead of as an ineffectual attempt to make a written one—upon which point I confess myself ignorant. Therefore"—and he tossed away his cigarette butt with an air of finality—"this letter bequeathing twenty-five thousand dollars to Sadie Burch—whoever and whatever she may be—is either an attempt to make a will or a codicil to a will in a way not recognized by the statute, or it is an attempt to add to, alter or vary a will already properly executed and witnessed by arbitrarily affixing to or placing within it an extraneous written paper."

"Well," commented Payson, "I understand what you've said about nun—nuncupative wills, all right,—that is, I think I do. But leaving them out of consideration I still don't see why this letter can't be regarded as *part* of the original will."

"For the reason that when your father executed the original document he went through every form required by the statute for making a will. If he hadn't, it wouldn't have been a will at all. If this paper, which never was witnessed by a single person, could be treated as a supplement or addition to the will, there would have been no use requiring the original will to be witnessed, either."

"That seems logical," agreed Payson. "But isn't it often customary to incorporate other papers by referring to them in a will?"

"It is sometimes done, and usually results in nothing but litigation. You see for yourself how absurd it would be to treat a paper drawn or executed after a will was made as part of it, for that would render the requirements of the statute nugatory."

"But suppose the letter was already in existence or was written at the same time as the will,—wouldn't that make a difference?" hesitated Payson.

"Not a bit! Not one bit!" chirped Tutt. "The law is settled that such a paper writing can be given effect only under certain very special conditions and only to a limited extent. Anyhow that question doesn't arise here."

"Why not?" queried the residuary legatee. "How do you know this letter wasn't written and placed inside the will when it was made?—And that my father supposed that of course it would be given effect?"

"In that case why shouldn't he have incorporated the legacy in the will?" countered Tutt sharply.

"He—er—may not have wished Mr. Tutt to know about it," murmured Payson, dropping his eyes.

"Oh,—hardly!" protested Tutt. "We can be morally certain that this letter was written and placed with the will that time your father came in here and asked to be allowed to see it, seven odd years ago. Mr. Tutt would have noticed it if your father had placed it with the will in the first instance and would have warned him that nothing of the sort could possibly be effective."

"But," insisted Payson, "assuming for argument's sake that this letter was in fact written at the time the will was originally executed, what is the reason the law won't recognize it as a valid bequest?"

Tutt smiled and fumbled in an open box for another cigarette.

"My dear sir," he replied, "no paper could possibly be treated as part of a will—even if extant at the time the will was executed—unless distinctly referred to in the will itself. In a word, there must be a clear and unmistakable intention on the part of the testator to attempt to incorporate the extraneous paper by reference. Now, here, there is no reference to the paper in the will at all."

"That is true!" admitted Payson. "But—"

"But even if there were," went on Tutt, eagerly, "the law is settled in this state that where a testator—either through carelessness or a desire to economize space or effort, has referred in his will to extraneous papers or memoranda, either as fixing the names of beneficiaries of particular devises or bequests, or as fixing the amount or the manner in which the amount of such devises or bequests is to be ascertained, such a paper must not contain any testamentary disposition of property. In a word the testator having willed something can *identify* it by means of an extraneous paper if properly designated, but he cannot *will* the thing away by an extraneous paper no matter how referred to. For example, if A wills to B 'all the stock covered by my agreement of May 1, with X' it merely describes and identifies the thing bequeathed,—and that is all right. The law will give effect to the identifying agreement, although it is separate from the will and unattested. But, if A's will read 'and I give such further bequests as appear in a paper filed herewith' and the paper contained a bequest to B of 'all the stock covered by my agreement of May 1, with X' it would be an attempted bequest outside of the will and so have no legal effect."

"Thanks," said Payson. "I understand. So in no event whatever could this letter have any legal effect?"

"Absolutely none whatever!—You're perfectly safe!" And Tutt leaned back with a comfortable smile.

But Payson did not smile in return. Neither was he comfortable. Be it said for him that, however many kinds of a fool he may have been, while momentarily relieved at knowing that he had no legal obligation to carry out his father's wishes so far as Sadie Burch was concerned, his conscience was by no means easy and he had not liked at all the tone in which the paunchy little lawyer had used the phrase "you're perfectly safe."

"What do you mean by 'perfectly safe'," he inquired rather coldly.

"Why, that Sadie Burch could never make you pay her the legacy—because it isn't a legal legacy. You can safely keep it. It's yours, legally and morally."

"Well, is it?" asked Payson slowly. "Morally, isn't it my duty to pay over the money, no matter who she is?"

Tutt, who had tilted backward in his swivel chair, brought both his feet to the floor with a bang.

"Of course it isn't!" he cried. "You'd be crazy to pay the slightest attention to any such vague and unexplained scrawl. Listen, young man! In the first place you haven't any idea when your father wrote that paper—except that it was at least seven years ago. He may have changed his mind a dozen times since he wrote it. It may have been a mere passing whim or fancy, done in a moment of weakness or emotion or temporary irrationality. Indeed, it may have been made under duress. Nobody but a lawyer who has the most intimate knowledge of his clients' daily life and affairs has the remotest suspicion of—Oh, well, we won't go into that! But, the first proposition is that in no event is it possible for you to say that the request in that letter was the actual wish of your father at the time of his death. All you can say is that at some time or other it may have been his wish."

"I see!" agreed Payson. "Well, what other points are there?"

"Secondly," continued Tutt, "it must be presumed that if your father took the trouble to retain a lawyer to have his will properly drawn and executed he must have known first, that it was necessary to do so in order to have his wishes carried out, and second, that no wish not properly incorporated in the will itself could have any legal effect. In other words, inferentially, he knew that this paper had no force and therefore it must be assumed that if he made it that way he intended that it should have no legal effect and did not intend that it should be carried out. Get me?"

"Why, yes, I think I do. Your point is that if a man knows the law and does a thing so it has no legal effect he should be assumed to intend that it have no legal effect."

"Exactly," Tutt nodded with satisfaction. "The law is wise, based on generations of experience. It realizes the uncertainties, vagaries, and vacillations of the human mind—and the opportunities afforded to designing people to take advantage of the momentary weaknesses of others—and hence to prevent fraud and insure that only the actual final wishes of a man shall be carried out it requires that those wishes shall be expressed in a particular, definite and formal way—in writing, signed and published before witnesses."

"You certainly make it very clear!" assented Payson. "What do executors usually do under such circumstances?"

"If they have sense they leave matters alone and let the law take its course," answered Tutt with conviction. "I've known of more trouble—! Several instances right here in this office. A widow found a paper with her husband's will expressing a wish that a certain amount of money should be given to a married woman living out in Duluth. There was nothing to indicate when the paper was written, although the will was executed only a month before he died. Apparently the deceased hadn't seen the lady in question for years. I told her to forget it, but nothing would suit her but that she should send the woman a money order for the full amount—ten thousand dollars. She kept it, all right! Well, the widow found out afterwards that her husband had written that paper thirty years before at a time when he was engaged to be married to that woman, that they had changed their minds and each had married happily and that the paper with some old love letters had, as usually happens, got mixed up with the will instead of having been destroyed as it should have been. You know, it's astonishing, the junk people keep in their safe deposit boxes! I'll bet that ninety-nine out of a hundred are half full of valueless and useless stuff, like old watches, grandpa's jet cuff buttons, the letters Uncle William wrote from the Holy Land, outlawed fire insurance and correspondence that nobody will ever read,—everything always gets mixed up together,—and yet every paper a man leaves after his death is a possible source of confusion or trouble. And one can't tell how or why a person at a particular time may come to express a wish in writing. It would be most dangerous to pay attention to it. Suppose it was *not* in writing. Morally, a wish is just as binding if spoken as if incorporated in a letter. Would you waste any time on Sadie Burch if she came in here and told you that your father had expressed the desire that she should have twenty-five thousand dollars? Not much!"

"I don't suppose so!" admitted Payson.

"Another thing!" said Tutt. "Remember this, the law would not *permit* you as executor of your father's will to pay over this money, if any other than yourself were the residuary legatee. You'd have no right to take twenty-five thousand dollars out of the estate and give it to Miss Burch at the expense of anybody else!"

"Then you say the law won't let me pay this money to Sadie Burch whether I am willing to or not?" asked Payson.

"Not as executor. As executor you're absolutely obliged to carry out the terms of the will and disregard anything else. You must preserve the estate intact and turn it over unimpaired to the residuary legatee!" repeated Tutt.

"But I am the residuary legatee!" said Payson.

"As executor you've got to pay it over in full to yourself as residuary legatee!" repeated Tutt stubbornly, evading the issue.

"Well, where does that leave me?" asked his client.

"It gets you out of your difficulty, doesn't it?" asked Tutt. "Don't borrow trouble! Don't—if you'll pardon my saying so—be an idiot!"

There was silence for several minutes, finally broken by the lawyer who came back again to the charge with renewed vigor.

"Why, this sort of thing comes up all the time. Take this sort of a case, for instance. The law only lets a man will away a certain proportion of his property to charity—says it isn't right for him to do so, if he leaves a family. Now suppose your father had given all his property to charity, would you feel obliged to impoverish yourself for the benefit of a Home for Aged Mariners?"

"Really," replied the bewildered Payson. "I don't know. But anyway I'm satisfied you're quite right and I'm tremendously obliged. However," he added musingly, "I'd rather like to know who this Sadie Burch is!"

"If I were you, young man," advised the lawyer sagely, "I wouldn't try to find out!"

Mr. Payson Clifford left the offices of Tutt & Tutt more recalcitrant against fate and irritated with his family than when he had entered them. He had found himself much less comfortably provided for than he had expected, and the unpleasant impression created by the supposed paternal relatives at his father's funeral had been heightened by the letter regarding Sadie Burch. There was something even more offensively plebeian about them than that of the vulgar Weng. It would have been bad enough to have had to consider the propriety of paying over a large sum to a lady calling herself by an elegant or at least debonair name like Claire Desmond or Lillian Lamar,—but Sadie! And Burch! Ye gods! It was ignoble, sordid. That was a fine discovery to make about one's father!

As he walked slowly up Fifth Avenue to his hotel it must be confessed that his reflections upon that father's memory were far from filial. He told himself that he'd always suspected something furtive about the old man, who must have been under most unusual and extraordinary obligations to a woman to whom he desired his son to turn over twenty-five thousand dollars. It was pretty nearly half of his entire fortune! Would cut down his income from around four thousand to nearly two thousand! The more he pondered upon the matter the more the lawyer's arguments seemed absolutely convincing. Lawyers knew more than other people about such things, anyway. You paid them for their advice, and he would doubtless have to pay Tutt for his upon this very subject, which, somehow, seemed to be rather a good reason for following it. No, he would dismiss Sadie Burch and the letter forever from his mind. Very likely she was dead anyway, whoever she was. Four thousand a year! Not a bad income for a bachelor!

And while our innocent young Launcelot trudging uptown hardened his heart against Sadie Burch, by chance that lady figured in a short but poignant conversation between Mr. Ephraim Tutt and Miss Minerva Wiggin on the threshold of the room from which he had just departed.

Miss Wiggin never trusted anybody but herself to lock up the offices, not even Mr. Tutt, and upon this particular evening she had made this an excuse to linger on after the others had gone home and waylay him. Such encounters were by no means infrequent and usually had a bearing upon the ethical aspect of some proposed course of legal procedure on the part of the firm.

Miss Minerva regarded Samuel Tutt as morally an abandoned and hopeless creature. Mr. Ephraim Tutt she loved with a devotion rare among a sex with whom devotion is happily a common trait, but there was a maternal quality in her affection accounted for by the fact that although Mr. Tutt was, to be sure, an old man in years, he had occasionally an elfin, Puck-like perversity which was singularly boyish, at which times she felt it obligatory for her own self-respect to call him to order. Thus, whenever Tutt seemed to be incubating some evasion of law which seemed more subtly plausible than ordinary she made it a point to call it to Mr. Tutt's attention. Also, whenever, as in the present case, she felt that by following the advice given by the junior member of the firm a client was about to embark upon some dubious enterprise or questionable course of conduct she endeavored to counteract his influence by appealing to the head of the firm.

During the interview between Tutt and Payson Clifford the door had been open and she had heard all of it; moreover, after Payson had gone away Tutt had called her in and gone over the situation with her. And she regarded Tutt's advice to his client,—not the purely legal aspect of it, but the personal and persuasive part of it,—as an interference with that young gentleman's freedom of conscience.

"Dear me!—I didn't know you were still here, Minerva!" exclaimed her employer as she confronted him in the outer office. "Is anything worrying you?"

"Not dangerously!" she replied with a smile. "And perhaps it's none of my business—"

"My business is thy business, my dear!" he answered. "Without you Tutt & Tutt would not be Tutt & Tutt. My junior partner may be the eyes and legs of the firm and I may be some other portion of its anatomy, but you are its heart and its conscience. Out with it! What rascality portends? What bird of evil omen hovers above the offices of Tutt & Tutt? Spare not an old man bowed down with the sorrows of this world! Has my shrewd associate counseled the robbing of a bank or the kidnapping from a widowed mother of her orphaned child?"

"Nothing quite so bad as that!" she retorted. "It's merely that Mr. Samuel Tutt used his influence this afternoon to try to persuade a young man not to carry out his father's wishes—expressed in a legally ineffective way—and I think he succeeded—although I'm not quite sure."

"That must have been Payson Clifford," answered Mr. Tutt. "What were the paternal wishes?"

"Mr. Tutt found a letter with the will in which the father asked the son to give twenty-five thousand dollars to a Miss Sadie Burch."

"Miss Sadie Burch!" repeated Mr. Tutt. "And who is she?"

"Nobody knows," said Miss Wiggin. "But whoever she is, our responsibility stops with advising Mr. Payson Clifford that the letter has no legal effect. Mr. Tutt went further and tried to induce Mr. Clifford not to respect the request contained in it. That, it seems to me, is going too far. Don't you think so?"

"Are you certain you never heard of this Miss Burch?" suddenly asked Mr. Tutt, peering at her sharply from beneath his shaggy eyebrows.

"Never," she replied.

"H'm!" ejaculated Mr. Tutt. "A woman in the case!"

"What sort of a young fellow is this Payson Clifford?" inquired Miss Wiggin after a moment.

"Oh, not so much of a much!" answered Mr. Tutt whimsically.

"And what was the father like?" she continued with a woman's curiosity.

"He wasn't so much of a much, either, evidently," answered Mr. Tutt.

We have previously had occasion to comment upon the fact that no client, male or female, consults a lawyer with regard to what he ought to do. Women, often having decided to do that which they ought not to do, attempt to secure counsel's approval of the contemplated sin; but while a lawyer is sometimes called upon to bolster up a guilty conscience, rarely is he sincerely invited to act as spiritual adviser. Most men being worse than their lawyers, prefer not to have the latter find them out. If they have made up their minds to do a mean thing they do not wish to run the chance of having their lawyer shame them out of it. That is their own business. And it should be! The law presents sufficiently perplexing problems for the lawyer without his seeking trouble in the dubious complexities of his client's morals! Anyhow, that is the regulation way a lawyer looks at it and that is the way to hold one's clients. Do what you are instructed to do—so long as it isn't too raw! Question the propriety of his course and while your client may follow your advice in this single instance he probably will not return again.

The paradoxical aspect of the matter with Mr. Tutt was that while he was known as a criminal lawyer whenever he was asked for advice he concerned himself quite as much with his client's moral as his legal duty. The rather subtle reason for this was probably to be found in the fact that since he found the law so easy to circumvent he preferred to disregard it entirely as a sanction of conduct and merely to ask himself "Now is this what a sportsman and a gentleman would do?" The fact that a man was a technical criminal meant nothing to him at all; what interested him was whether the man was or was not a "mean" man. If he was, to hell with him! In a word, he applied to any given situation the law as it ought to be and not the law as it was. A very easy and flexible test! say you, sarcastically. Do you really think so? There may be forty different laws upon the same subject in as many different states of our political union, but how many differing points of view upon any single moral question would you find among as many citizens? The moral code of decent people is practically the same all over the terrestrial ball, and fundamentally it has not changed since the days of Hammurabi. The ideas of gentlemen and sportsmen as to what "is done" and "isn't done" haven't changed since Fabius Tullius caught snipe in the Pontine marshes.

Mr. Tutt was a crank on this general subject and he carried his enthusiasm so far that he was always tilting like Don Quixote at some imaginary windmill, dragging a very unwilling Sancho Panza after him in the form of his reluctant partner. Moreover, he had a very keen sympathy for all kinds of outcasts, deeming most of them victims of the sins of their own or somebody's else fathers. So when he learned from Miss Wiggin that Tutt had presumed to interfere with the financial prospects of the unknown Miss Sadie Burch he was distinctly aggrieved, less on her account to be sure than upon that of his client's whom he regarded more or less in his keeping. And, as luck would have it, the object of his grievance, having forgotten something, at that moment unexpectedly reentered the office to retrieve it.

"Hello, Mr. Tutt!" he exclaimed. "Not gone yet!"

His senior partner glanced at him sharply, while Miss Wiggin hastily sidestepped into the corridor.

"Look here, Tutt!" said Mr. Tutt. "I don't know just what you've been telling young Clifford, or how you've been interfering in his private affairs, but if you've been persuading him to disregard any wish of his father plainly expressed in his own handwriting and incorporated with his will you've gone further than you've any right to go."

"But," expostulated Tutt, "you know how dangerous it is to meddle with things like that. Our experience certainly shows that it's far wiser to let the law settle all doubtful questions than to try to guess what the final testamentary intention of a dead testator really was. Don't you remember the Dodworth case? A hypersensitive conscience cost our widowed client ten thousand dollars! I say, leave well enough alone."

"'Well enough'! 'Well enough'!" snarled Mr. Tutt. "Are you going to constitute yourself the judge of what is well enough for a young man's soul? I give you fair warning, Tutt: he's heard your side of it, but before he gets through he's going to hear mine as well!"

Samuel Tutt turned a faint pink in the region of his collar.

"Why, certainly, Mr. Tutt!" he stammered. "Do so, by all means!"

"You jolly well bet I will!" replied Mr. Tutt, jamming on his stovepipe.

Several days passed, however, without the subject being mentioned further, while the proper steps to probate the will were taken as usual. Payson Clifford's dilemma had no legal reaction. He had made up his mind and he was going to stick to it. He had taken the opinion of counsel and was fully satisfied with what he had done. Nobody was going to know anything about it, anyway. When the proper time came he would burn the Sadie Burch letter and forget Sadie Burch. That is, he thought he was going to and that he could. But—as Plautus says: "*Nihil est miserius quam animus hominis conscius.*"

You see, Payson Clifford, having been sent to a decent school and a decent college, irrespective of whether his father was a rotter or not, had imbibed something of a sense of honor. Struggle as he would against it, the shadow of Sadie Burch kept creeping athwart his mind. There were so many possibilities! Suppose she was in desperate straits? Hadn't he better look her up, anyhow? No, he most definitely didn't want to know anything about her! Supposing she really had rendered some service to his father for which she ought to be repaid as he had sought to repay her? These thoughts obtruded themselves upon Payson's attention when he least desired it, but they did not cause him to alter his intention to get his hooks into his father's whole residuary estate and keep it for himself. He had, you observe, a conscience, but it couldn't stand up against twenty-five thousand dollars reinforced by perfectly sound legal arguments.

No, he had a good excuse for not being a gentleman and a sportsman and he did not purpose to look for any reasons for doing differently. Then unexpectedly he was invited to dinner by Mr. Ephraim Tutt in a funny old ramshackle house on West Twenty-third Street with ornamented iron piazza railings all covered with the withered stalks of long dead wistarias, and something happened to him. "Payson Clifford's Twenty-five Thousand Dollar Dinner." He had no suspicion, of course, what was coming to him when he went there,—went, merely because Mr. Tutt was one of the very few friends of his father that he knew. And he held towards the old lawyer rather the same sort of patronizing attitude that he had had towards the old man. It would be a rotten dinner probably followed by a deadly dull evening with a snuffy old fossil who would tell him long-winded, rambling anecdotes of what New York had been like when there were wild goats in Central Park.

The snuffy old fossil, however, made no reference whatever to either old New York or wild goats,—the nearest he came to it being wild oats. Instead he began the dreary evening by opening a cupboard on his library wall and disclosing three long bottles, from which he partially filled a shining silver receptacle containing cracked ice. This he shook with astonishing skill and vigor, meantime uttering loud outcries of "Miranda! Fetch up the mint!" Then a buxom colored lady in calico—with a grin like that which made Aunt Sallie famous—having appeared, panting, with two large glasses and a bundle of green herbage upon a silver salver, the old fossil poured out a seething decoction—of which like only the memory remains—performed an incantation over each glass with the odoriferous greens, smiled fondly upon the work of his hands and remarked with amiable hospitality, "Well, my son! Glad to see you!—Here's how!"

Almost immediately a benign animal magnetism pervaded the bosom of Payson Clifford, and from his bosom reached out through his arteries and veins, his arterioles and venioles, to the uttermost ends of his being. He perceived in an instant that Mr. Tutt was no ordinary man and his house no ordinary house; and this impression was intensified when, seated at his host's shining mahogany table with its heavy cut glass and queer old silver, he discovered that Miranda was no ordinary cook. He began to be inflated over having discovered this Mr. Tutt, who pressed succulent oysters and terrapin stew upon him, accompanied by a foaming bottle of Krug '98. He found himself possessed of an astounding appetite and a prodigious thirst. The gas lights in the old bronze chandelier shone like a galaxy of radiant suns above his head and warmed him through and through. And after the terrapin Miranda brought in a smoking wild turkey with two quail roasted inside of it, and served with currant jelly, rice cakes, and sweet potatoes fried in melted sugar. Then, as in a dream, he heard a soul-satisfying pop and Miranda placed a tall, amber glass at his wrist and filled it with the creaming redrose wine of ancient Burgundy. He heard himself telling Mr. Tutt all about himself,—the most intimate secrets of his heart,—and saw Mr. Tutt listening attentively, almost reverently. He perceived that he was making an astonishing impression upon Mr. Tutt who obviously thought him a great man; and after keeping him in reasonable doubt about it for awhile he modestly admitted to Mr. Tutt that this was so. Then he drank several more glasses of Burgundy and ate an enormous pile of waffles covered with maple syrup. "I'se in town, honey!" Mr. Tutt had grown several sizes larger—the whole room was full of him. Lastly he had black coffee and some port. It was an occasion, he asserted,—er—always goo' weather,—or somethin'—when goo' fellows got together! He declared with an emphasis which was quite unnecessary, but which, however, did not disturb him, that there were too few men like themselves in the world,—men with the advantage of education,—men of ideals. He told Mr. Tutt that he loved him. He no longer had a father, and, evidently relying on further similar entertainments, he wanted Mr. Tutt for one. Mr. Tutt generously assented to act in that capacity and as the first step assisted his guest upstairs to the library where he opened the window a few inches.

Presently, Payson did not know how exactly, they got talking all about life,—and Mr. Tutt said ruminatively that after all the only things that really counted were loyalty and courage and kindness,—and that a little human sympathy extended even in what sometimes seemed at first glance the wrong direction often did more good—made more for real happiness—than the most efficient organized charity. He spoke of the loneliness of age—the inevitable loneliness of the human soul,—the thirst for daily affection. And then they drifted off to college, and Mr. Tutt inquired casually if Payson had seen much of his father, who, he took occasion to remark, had been a good type of straightforward, honest, hard-working business man.

Payson, smoking his third cigar, and taking now and then a dash of cognac, began to think better of his old dad. He really hadn't paid him quite the proper attention. He admitted it to Mr. Tutt—with the first genuine tears in his eyes since he had left Cambridge;—perhaps, if he had been more to him—. But Mr. Tutt veered off again—this time on university education; the invaluable function of the university being, he said, to preserve intact and untarnished in a materialistic age the spiritual ideals inherited from the past.

In this rather commonplace sentiment Payson agreed with him passionately. He further agreed with equal enthusiasm when his host advanced the doctrine that after all to preserve one's honor stainless was the only thing that much mattered. Absolutely! declared Payson, as he allowed Mr. Tutt to press another glass of port upon him.

Payson, in spite of the slight beading of his forehead and the blurr about the gas jets, began to feel very much the man of the world,—not a "six bottle man" perhaps, but—and he laughed complacently—a "two bottle man." If he'd lived back in the good old sporting days very likely he could have done better. But he's taken care of two full bottles, hadn't he? Mr. Tutt replied that he'd taken care of them very well indeed. And with this opening the old lawyer launched into his favorite topic,—to wit, that there were only two sorts of men in the world—

gentlemen, and those who were not. What made a man a gentleman was gallantry and loyalty,—the readiness to sacrifice everything—even life—to an ideal. The hero was the chap who never counted the cost to himself. That was why people revered the saints, acclaimed the cavalier, and admired the big-hearted gambler who was ready to stake his fortune on the turn of a card. There was even, he averred, an element of spirituality in the gambler's carelessness about money.

This theory greatly interested Payson, who held strongly with it, having always had a secret, sneaking fondness for gamblers. On the strength of it he mentioned Charles James Fox—there was a true gentleman and sportsman for you! No mollycoddle—but a roaring, six bottle fellow—with a big brain and a scrupulous sense of honor. Yes, sir! Charley Fox was the right sort! He managed to intimate successfully that Charley and he were very much the same breed of pup. At this point Mr. Tutt, having carefully committed his guest to an ethical standard as far removed as possible from one based upon self-interest, opened the window a few more inches, sauntered over to the mantel, lit a fresh stogy and spread his long legs in front of the sea-coal fire like an elongated Colossus of Rhodes. He commenced his dastardly countermining of his partner's advice by complimenting Payson on being a man whose words, manner and appearance proclaimed him to the world a true sport and a regular fellow. From which flattering prologue he slid naturally into said regular fellow's prospects and aims in life. He trusted that Payson Clifford, Senior, had left a sufficient estate to enable Payson, Junior, to complete his education at Harvard?—He forgot, he confessed just what the residue amounted to. Then he turned to the fire, kicked it, knocked the ash off the end of his stogy and waited—in order to give his guest a chance to come to himself,—for Mr. Payson Clifford had suddenly turned a curious color, due to the fact that he was unexpectedly confronted with the necessity of definitely deciding then and there whether he was going to line up with the regular fellows or the second raters, the gentlemen or the cads, the C.J. Foxes or the Benedict Arnolds of mankind. He wasn't wholly the real thing, a conceited young ass, if you choose, but on the other hand he wasn't by any means a bad sort. In short, he was very much like all the rest of us. And he wasn't ready to sign the pledge just yet. He realized that he had put himself at a disadvantage, but he wasn't going to commit himself until he had had a good chance to think it all over carefully. In thirty seconds he was sober as a judge—and a sober judge at that.

"Mr. Tutt," he said in quite a different tone of voice. "I've been talking pretty big, I guess,—bigger than I really am. The fact is I've got a problem of my own that's bothering me a lot."

Mr. Tutt nodded understandingly.

"You mean Sadie Burch."

"Yes."

"Well, what's the problem? Your father wanted you to give her the money, didn't he?"

Payson hesitated. What he was about to say seemed so disingenuous, even though it had originated with Tutt & Tutt.

"How do I know really what he wanted? He may have changed his mind a dozen times since he put it with his will."

"If he had he wouldn't have left it there, would he?" asked Mr. Tutt with a smile.

"But perhaps he forgot all about it,—didn't remember that it was there," persisted the youth, still clinging desperately to the lesser Tutt. "And, if he hadn't would have torn it up."

"That might be equally true of the provisions of his will, might it not?" countered the lawyer.

"But," squirmed Payson, struggling to recall Tutt's arguments, previously so convincing, "he knew how a will ought to be executed and as he deliberately neglected to execute the paper in a legal fashion, isn't it fair to presume that he did not intend it to have any legal force?"

"Yes," replied Mr. Tutt with entire equanimity, "I agree with you that it is fair to assume that he did not intend it to have any legal effect."

"Well, then!" exclaimed Payson exultantly.

"But," continued the lawyer, "that does not prove that he did not intend it to have a moral effect,—and expect you to honor and respect his wishes, just as if he had whispered them to you with his dying breath."

There was something in his demeanor which, while courteous, had a touch of severity, that made Payson feel abashed. He perceived that he could not afford to let Mr. Tutt think him a cad,—when he was really a C.J. Fox. And in his mental floundering his brain came into contact with the only logical straw in the entire controversy.

"Ah!" he said with an assumption of candor. "In that case I should know positively that they were in fact my father's wishes."

"Exactly!" replied Mr. Tutt. "And you'd carry them out without a moment's hesitation."

"Of course!" yielded Payson.

"Then the whole question is whether or not this paper does express a wish of his. That problem is a real problem, and it is for you alone to solve,—and, of course, you're under the disadvantage of having a financial interest in the result, which makes it doubly hard."

"All the same," maintained the boy, "I want to be fair to myself."

"—And to him," added Mr. Tutt solemnly. "The fact that this wish is not expressed in such a way as to be legally obligatory makes it all the more binding. In a way, I suppose, that is your hard luck. You might, perhaps, fight a provision in the will. You can't fight this—or disregard it, either."

"I don't exactly see why this is any *more* binding than a provision in the will itself!" protested Payson.

Mr. Tutt threw his stogy into the fire and fumbled for another in the long box on the library table.

"Maybe it isn't," he conceded, "but I've always liked that specious anecdote attributed to Sheridan who paid his gambling debts and let his tailor wait. You remember it, of course? When the tailor demanded the reason for this Sheridan told him that a gambling debt was a debt of honor and a tailor's bill was not, since his fortunate adversary at the card table had only his promise to pay, whereas the tailor possessed an action for an account which he could prosecute in the courts.

"'In that case!' declared the tailor, 'I'll tear up my bill!' which he did, and Sheridan thereupon promptly paid him. Have another nip of brandy?"

"No, thank you!" answered Payson. "It's getting late and I must be going. I've—I've had a perfectly—er—ripping time!"

"You must come again soon!" said Mr. Tutt warmly, from the top of the steps outside.

As Payson reached the sidewalk he looked back somewhat shamefacedly and said:

"Do you think it makes any difference what sort of a person this Sadie Burch is?"

In the yellow light of the street lamp it seemed to the collegian as if the face of the old man bore for an instant a fleeting resemblance to that of his father.

"Not one particle!" he answered. "Good night, my boy!"

But Payson Clifford did not have a good night by any manner of means. Instead of returning to his hotel he wandered aimless and miserable along the river front. He no longer had any doubt as to his duty. Mr. Tutt had demolished Tutt in a breath,—and put the whole proposition clearly. Tutt had given, as it were, and Mr. Tutt had taken away. However, he told himself, that wasn't all there was to it; the money was his in law and no one could deprive him of it. Why not sit tight and let Mr. Tutt go to the devil? He need never see him again! And no one else would ever know! Twenty-five thousand dollars? It would take him years to earn such a staggering sum! Besides, there were two distinct sides to the question. Wasn't Tutt just as good a lawyer as Mr. Tutt? Couldn't he properly decide in favor of himself when the court was equally divided? And Tutt had said emphatically that he would be a fool to surrender the money. As Payson Clifford trudged along the shadows of the docks he became obsessed with a curious feeling that Tutt and Mr. Tutt were both there before him; Mr. Tutt—a tall, benevolent figure carrying a torch in the shape of a huge, black, blazing stogy that beckoned him onward through the darkness; and behind him Tutt—a little paunchy red devil with horns and a tail—who tweaked him by the coat and twittered, "Don't throw away twenty-five thousand dollars! The best way is to leave matters as they are and let the law settle everything. Then you take no chances!"

But in the end—along about a quarter to seven A.M.—Mr. Tutt won. Exhausted, but at peace with himself, Payson Clifford stumbled into the Harvard Club on Forty-fourth Street, ordered three fried eggs done on one side, two orders of bacon and a pot of coffee, and then wrote a letter which he dispatched by a messenger to Tutt & Tutt.

"Gentlemen," it read: "Will you kindly take immediate steps to find Miss Sarah Burch and pay over to her twenty-five thousand dollars from my father's residuary estate. I am entirely satisfied that this was his wish. I am returning to Cambridge to-day. If necessary you can communicate with me there.

"Yours very truly,

"PAYSON CLIFFORD."

One might suppose that a legatee to twenty-five thousand dollars could be readily found; but Miss Sadie Burch proved a most elusive person. No Burches grew in Hoboken—according to either the telephone or the business directory—and Mr. Tutt's repeated advertisements in the newspapers of that city elicited no response. Three months went by and it began to look as if the lady had either died or permanently absented herself—and that Payson Clifford might be able to keep his twenty-five thousand with a clear conscience. Then one day in May came a letter from a small town in the central part of New Jersey from Sadie Burch. She had, she said, only just learned entirely by accident that she was an object of interest to Messrs. Tutt & Tutt. Unfortunately, it was not convenient for her to come to New York City, but if she could be of any service to them she would be pleased, etc.

"I think I'll give the lady the once-over!" remarked Mr. Tutt, as he looked across the glittering bay to the shadowy hills of New Jersey. "It's a wonderful day, and there isn't much to do here...."

"Sadie Burch? Sadie Burch? Sure, I know her!" answered the lanky man driving the flivver tractor nearby, as he inspected the motor carrying Mr. Tutt. "She lives in the second house beyond the big elm—" and he started plowing again with a great clatter.

The road glared white in the late afternoon sun. On either side stretched miles of carefully cultivated fields, the country drowsed, the air hot, but sweet with magnolia, lilac and apple blossoms. Miss Burch had obviously determined that when she retired from the world of men she would make a thorough job of it and expose herself to no temptation to return—eight miles from the nearest railroad. Just beyond the elms they slowed up alongside a white picket fence enclosing an old-fashioned garden whence came to Mr. Tutt the busy murmur of bees. Then they came to a gate that opened upon a red-tiled, box-bordered, moss-grown walk, leading to a small white house with blue and white striped awnings. A green and gold lizard poked its head out of the hedge and eyed Mr. Tutt rather with curiosity than hostility.

"Does Miss Sadie Burch live here?" asked Mr. Tutt of the lizard.

"Yes!" answered a cheerful female voice from the veranda. "Won't you come up on the piazza?"

The voice was not the kind of voice Mr. Tutt had imagined as belonging to Sadie Burch. But neither was the lady on the piazza that kind of lady. In the shadow of the awning in a comfortable rocking chair sat a white-haired, kindly-faced woman, knitting a baby jacket. She looked up at him with a friendly smile.

"I'm Miss Burch," she said. "I suppose you're that lawyer I wrote to? Won't you come up and sit down?"

"Thanks," he replied, drawing nearer with an answering smile. "I can only stay a few moments and I've been sitting in the motor most of the day. I might as well come to the point at once. You have doubtless heard of the death of Mr. Payson Clifford, Senior?"

Miss Burch laid down the baby-jacket and her lips quivered. Then the tears welled in her faded blue eyes and she fumbled hastily in her bosom for her handkerchief.

"You must excuse me!" she said in a choked voice. "—Yes, I read about it. He was the best friend I had in the world,—except my brother John. The kindest, truest friend that ever lived!"

She looked out across the little garden and wiped her eyes again.

Mr. Tutt sat down upon the moss-covered door-step beside her.

"I always thought he was a good man," he returned quietly. "He was an old client of mine—although I didn't know him very well."

"I owe this house to him," continued Miss Burch tenderly. "If it hadn't been for Mr. Clifford I don't know what would have become of me. Now that John is dead and I'm all alone in the world this little place—with the flowers and the bees—is all I've got."

They were silent for several moments. Then Mr. Tutt said:

"No, it isn't all. Mr. Clifford left a letter with his will in which he instructed his son to pay you twenty-five thousand dollars. I'm here to give it to you."

A puzzled look came over her face, and then she smiled again and shook her head.

"That was just like him!" she remarked. "But it's all a mistake. He paid me back that money five years ago. You see he persuaded John to go into some kind of a business scheme with him and they lost all they put into it—twenty-five thousand apiece. It was all we had. It wasn't his fault, but after John died Mr. Clifford made me—simply made me—let him give the money back. He must have written the letter before that and forgotten all about it!"

You're Another!

"We have strict statutes, and most biting laws."
Measure for Measure, Act I, Scene 4.

"I am further of opinion that it would be better for us to have [no laws] at all than to have them in so prodigious numbers as we have."
—Montaigne. Of Experience, Chapter XIII.

Mrs. Pierpont Pumpelly, lawful spouse of Vice President Pumpelly, of Cuban Crucible, erstwhile of Athens, Ohio, was fully conscious that even if she wasn't the smartest thing on Fifth Avenue, her snappy little car was. It was, as she said, a "perfec' beejew!" The two robes of silver fox alone had cost eighty-five hundred dollars, but that was nothing; Mrs. Pumpelly—in her stockings—cost Pierpont at least ten times that every year. But he could afford it with Cruce at 791. So, having moved from Athens to the metropolis, they had a glorious time. Out home the Pierpont had been simply a P. and no questions asked as to what it stood for; P. Pumpelly. But whatever its past the P. had now blossomed definitely into Pierpont.

Though the said Pierpont produced the wherewithal, it was his wife, Edna, who attended to the disbursing of it. She loved her husband, but regarded him socially as somewhat of a liability, and Society was now, as she informed everybody, her "meal yure."

She had eaten her way straight through the meal—opera box, pew at St. Simeon Stylites, Crystal Room, musicales, Carusals, hospital entertainments, Malted Milk for Freezing France, Inns for Indigent Italians, Biscuits for Bereft Belgians, dinner parties, lunch parties, supper parties, the whole thing; and a lot of the right people had come, too.

The fly in the ointment of her social happiness—and unfortunately it happened to be an extremely gaudy butterfly indeed—was her next-door neighbor, Mrs. Rutherford Wells, who obstinately refused to recognize her existence.

At home, in Athens, Edna would have resorted to the simple expedient of sending over the hired girl to borrow something. But here there was nothing doing. Mrs. Rutherford had probably never seen her own chef and Mrs. Pumpelly was afraid of hers. Besides, even Edna recognized the lamentable fact that it was up to Mrs. Wells to call first, which she didn't. Once when the ladies had emerged simultaneously from their domiciles Mrs. Pumpelly had smilingly waddled forward a few steps with an ingratiating bow, but Mrs. Wells had looked over her head and hadn't seen her.

Thereupon the iron had entered into Mrs. Pumpelly's soul and her life had become wormwood and gall, ashes in her mouth and all the rest of it. She proposed to get even with the cat at the very first chance, but somehow the chance never seemed to come. She hated to be living on the same street with that kind of nasty person. And who was this Wells woman? Her husband never did a thing except play croquet or something at a club! He probably was a drunkard—and a roo-ay. Mrs. Pumpelly soon convinced herself that Mrs. Wells also must be a very undesirable, if not hopelessly immoral lady. Anyhow, she made up her mind that she would certainly take nothing further from her. Even if Mrs. Wells should have a change of heart and see fit to call, she just wouldn't return it! So when she rolled up in the diminutive car and found Mrs. Wells' lumbering limousine blocking the doorway she was simply furious.

"Make that man move along!" she directed, and Jules honked and honked, but the limousine did not budge.

Then Mrs. Pumpelly gave way to a fit of indignation that would have done her proud even in Athens, Ohio. Fire-breathing, she descended from her car and, approaching the limousine, told the imperturbable chauffeur that even if he did work for Mrs. Rutherford Wells, Mrs. Rutherford Wells was no better than anybody else, and that gave him no right to block up the whole street. She spoke loudly, emphatically, angrily, and right in the middle of it the chauffeur, who had not deigned to look in her direction, slyly pressed the electric button of his horn and caused it to emit a low scornful grunt. Then a footman opened the door of the Wells mansion and Mrs. Rutherford Wells herself came down the steps, and Mrs. Pumpelly told her to her face exactly what she thought of her and ordered her to move her car along so her own could get in front of the vestibule.

Mrs. Wells ignored her. Deliberately—and as if there were no such person as Mrs. Pumpelly upon the sidewalk—she stepped into her motor and, the chauffeur having adjusted the robe, she remarked in a casual, almost indifferent manner that nevertheless made Mrs. Pumpelly squirm, "Go to Mr. Hepplewhite's, William. Pay no attention to that woman. If she makes any further disturbance call a policeman."

And the limousine rolled away with a sneer at Mrs. Pumpelly from the exhaust. More than one king has been dethroned for far less cause!

"You telephone Mr. Edgerton," she almost shrieked at Simmons, the butler, "that he should come right up here as fast as he can. I've got to see him at once!"

"Very good, madam," answered Simmons obsequiously.

And without more ado, in less than forty minutes, the distinguished Mr. Wilfred Edgerton, of Edgerton & Edgerton, attorneys for Cuban Crucible and hence alert to obey the behests of the wives of the officers thereof, had deposited his tall silk hat on the marble Renaissance table in the front hall and was entering Mrs. Pumpelly's Louis Quinze drawing-room with the air of a Sir Walter Raleigh approaching his Queen Elizabeth.

"Sit down, Mr. Edgerton!" directed the lady impressively. "No, you'll find that other chair more comfortable; the one you're in's got a hump in the seat. As I was saying to the butler before you came, I've been insulted and I propose to teach that woman she can't make small of me no matter what it costs—and Pierpont says you're no slouch of a charger at that."

"My dear madam!" stammered the embarrassed attorney. "Of course, there are lawyers and lawyers. But if you wish the best I feel sure my firm charges no more than others of equal standing. In any event you can be assured of our devotion to your interests. Now what, may I ask, are the circumstances of the case?"

"Mr. Edgerton," she began, "I just want you should listen carefully to what I have to say. This woman next door to me here has—"

At this point, as paper is precious and the lady voluble, we will drop the curtain upon the first act of our legal comedy.

"I suppose we'll have to do it for her!" growled Mr. Wilfred Edgerton to his brother on his return to their office. "She's a crazy idiot and I'm very much afraid we'll all get involved in a good deal of undesirable publicity. Still, she's the wife of the vice president of our best paying client!"

"What does she want us to do?" asked Mr. Winfred, the other Edgerton. "We can't afford to be made ridiculous—for anybody."

This was quite true since dignity was Edgerton & Edgerton's long suit, they being the variety of Wall Street lawyers who are said to sleep in their tall hats and cutaways.

"If you can imagine it," replied his brother irritably, "she insists on our having Mrs. Wells arrested for obstructing the street in front of her house. She asked me if it wasn't against the law, and I took a chance and told her it was. Then she wanted to start for the police court at once, but as I'd never been in one I said we'd have to prepare the papers; I didn't know what papers."

"But we can't arrest Mrs. Wells!" expostulated Mr. Winfred Edgerton. "She's socially one of our most prominent people. I dined with her only last week!"

By Advice of Counsel

"That's why Mrs. Pumpelly wants to have her arrested, I fancy!" replied Mr. Wilfred gloomily. "Mrs. Wells has given her the cold shoulder. It's no use; I tried to argue the old girl out of it, but I couldn't. She knows what she wants and she jolly well intends to have it."

"I wish you joy of her!" mournfully rejoined the younger Edgerton. "But it's your funeral. I can't help you. I never got anybody arrested and I haven't the least idea how to go about it."

"Neither have I," admitted his brother. "Luckily my practise has not been of that sort. However, it can't be a difficult matter. The main thing is to know exactly what we are trying to arrest Mrs. Wells for."

"Why don't you retain Tutt & Tutt to do it for us?" suggested Winfred. "Criminal attorneys are used to all that sort of rotten business."

"Oh, it wouldn't do to let Pumpelly suspect we couldn't handle it ourselves. Besides, the lady wants distinguished counsel to represent her. No, for once we've got to lay dignity aside. I think I'll send Maddox up to the Criminal Courts Building and have him find out just what to do."

It may seem remarkable that neither of the members of a high-class law firm in New York City should ever have been in a police court, but such a situation is by no means infrequent. The county or small-town attorney knows his business from the ground up. He starts with assault and battery, petty larceny and collection cases and gradually works his way up, so to speak, to murder and corporate reorganizations. But in Wall Street the young student whose ambition is to appear before the Supreme Court of the United States in some constitutional matter as soon as possible is apt to spend his early years in brief writing and then become a specialist in real estate, corporation, admiralty or probate law and perhaps never see the inside of a trial court at all, much less a police court, which, to the poor and ignorant, at any rate, is the most important court of any of them, since it is here that the citizen must go to enforce his everyday rights.

Mr. Wilfred Edgerton suspected that a magistrate's court was a dirty sort of hole, full of brawling shyster lawyers, and he didn't want to know any more about such places than he could help. Theoretically he was aware that on a proper complaint sworn to by a person supposing himself or herself criminally aggrieved the judge would issue a warrant to an officer, who would execute it on the person of the criminal and hale him or her to jail. The idea of Mrs. Wells being dragged shrieking down Fifth Avenue or being carted away from her house in a Black Maria filled him with dismay.

Yet that was what Mrs. Pumpelly proposed to have done, and unfortunately he had to do exactly what Mrs. Pumpelly said; quickly too.

"Maddox," he called to a timid youth in a green eye-shade sitting in lonely grandeur in the spacious library, "just run up to the—er—magistrate's court on Blank Street and ascertain the proper procedure for punishing a person for obstructing the highway. If you find an appropriate statute or ordinance you may lay an information against Mrs. Rutherford Wells for violating it this afternoon in front of the residence next to hers; and see that the proper process issues in the regular way."

To hear him one would have thought he did things like that daily before breakfast—such is the effect of legal jargon.

"Yes, sir," answered Maddox respectfully, making a note. "Do you wish to have the warrant held or executed?"

Mr. Wilfred Edgerton bit his mustache doubtfully.

"We-ell," he answered at length, perceiving that he stood upon the brink of a legal Rubicon, "you may do whatever seems advisable under all the circumstances."

In his nervous condition he did not recall what, had he stopped calmly to consider the matter, he must have known very well—namely, that no warrant could possibly issue unless Mrs. Pumpelly, as complainant, signed and swore to the information herself.

"Very well, sir," answered Maddox, in the same tone and manner that he would have used had he been a second footman at Mrs. Pumpelly's.

Thereafter both Edgertons, but particularly Wilfred, passed a miserable hour. They realized that they had started something and they had no idea of where, how or when what they had started would stop. Indeed they had terrifying visions of Mrs. Wells being beaten into insensibility, if not into a pulp, by a cohort of brutal police officers, and of their being held personally responsible. But before anything of that sort actually happened Maddox returned.

"Well," inquired Wilfred with an assumption of nonchalance, "what did you find out?"

"The magistrate said that we would have to apply at the court in the district where the offense occurred and that Mrs. Pumpelly would have to appear there in person. Obstructing a highway is a violation of Section Two of Article Two of the Police Department Regulations for Street Traffic, which reads: 'A vehicle waiting at the curb shall promptly give way to a vehicle arriving to take up or set down passengers.' It is not usual to issue a warrant in such cases, but a summons merely."

"Ah!" sighed both Edgertons in great relief.

"Upon which the defendant must appear in default of fine or imprisonment," continued Maddox.

The two lawyers looked at one another inquiringly.

"Did they treat you—er—with politeness?" asked Wilfred curiously.

"Oh, well enough," answered the clerk. "I can't say it's a place I hanker to have much to do with. It's not like an afternoon tea party. But it's all right. Do you wish me to do anything further?"

"Yes!" replied Wilfred with emphasis, "I do. I wish you would go right up to Mrs. Pumpelly's house, conduct that lady to the nearest police court and have her swear out the summons for Mrs. Wells herself. I'll telephone her that you are coming."

Which was a wise conclusion, in view of the fact that Edna Pumpelly, née Haskins, was much better equipped by nature to take care of Mr. Wilfred Edgerton in the hectic environs of a police court than he was qualified to take care of her. And so it was that just as Mrs. Rutherford Wells was about to sit down to tea with several fashionable friends her butler entered, bearing upon a salver a printed paper, which he presented to her, in manner and form the following:

CITY MAGISTRATE'S COURT, CITY OF NEW YORK

In the name of the people of the State of New York To "Jane" Wells, the name "Jane" being fictitious:

You are hereby summoned to appear before the ———— District Magistrate's Court, Borough of Manhattan, City of New York, on the eighth day of May, 1920, at ten o'clock in the forenoon, to answer the charge made against you by Edna Pumpelly for violation of Section Two, Article Two of the Traffic Regulations providing that a vehicle waiting at the curb shall promptly give way to a vehicle arriving to take up or set down passengers, and upon your failure to appear at the time and place herein mentioned you are liable to a fine of not exceeding fifty dollars or to imprisonment of not exceeding ten days or both.

Dated 6th day of May, 1920.

JAMES CUDDAHEY, Police Officer,

Police Precinct ————, New York City.

Attest: JOHN J. JONES, Chief City Magistrate.

"Heavens!" cried Mrs. Wells as she read this formidable document. "What a horrible woman! What shall I do?"

Mr. John De Puyster Hepplewhite, one of the nicest men in New York, who had himself once had a somewhat interesting experience in the criminal courts in connection with the arrest of a tramp who had gone to sleep in a pink silk bed in the Hepplewhite mansion on Fifth Avenue, smiled deprecatingly, set down his Dresden-china cup and dabbed his mustache decorously with a filigree napkin.

"Dear lady," he remarked with conviction, "in such distressing circumstances I have no hesitation whatever in advising you to consult Mr. Ephraim Tutt."

"I have been thinking over what you said the other day regarding the relationship of crime to progress, Mr. Tutt, and I'm rather of the opinion that it's rot," announced Tutt as he strolled across from his own office to that of his senior partner for a cup of tea at practically the very moment when Mr. Hepplewhite was advising Mrs. Wells. "In the vernacular—bunk."

"What did he say?" asked Miss Wiggin, rinsing out with hot water Tutt's special blue-china cup, in the bottom of which had accumulated some reddish-brown dust from Mason & Welsby's Admiralty and Divorce Reports upon the adjacent shelf.

"He made the point," answered Tutt, helping himself to a piece of toast, "that crime was—if I may be permitted to use the figure—part of the onward urge of humanity toward a new and perhaps better social order; a natural impulse to rebel against existing abuses; and he made the claim that though an unsuccessful revolutionary was of course regarded as a criminal, on the other hand, if successful he at once became a patriot, a hero, a statesman or a saint."

"A very dangerous general doctrine, I should say," remarked Miss Wiggin. "I should think it all depended on what sort of laws he was rebelling against. I don't see how a murderer could ever be regarded as assisting in the onward urge toward sweetness and light, exactly."

"Wouldn't it depend somewhat on whom you were murdering?" inquired Mr. Tutt, finally succeeding in his attempt to make a damp stogy continue in a state of combustion. "If you murdered a tyrant wouldn't you be contributing toward progress?"

"No," retorted Miss Wiggin, "you wouldn't; and you know it. In certain cases where the laws are manifestly unjust, antiquated or perhaps do not really represent the moral sense of the community their violation may occasionally call attention to their absurdity, like the famous blue laws of Connecticut, for example; but as the laws as a whole do crystallize the general opinion of what is right and desirable in matters of conduct a movement toward progress would be exhibited not by breaking laws but by making laws."

"But," argued Mr. Tutt, abandoning his stogy, "isn't the making of a new law the same thing as changing an old law? And isn't changing a law essentially the same thing as breaking it?"

"It isn't," replied Miss Wiggin tartly. "For the obvious and simple reason that the legislators who change the laws have the right to do so, while the man who breaks them has not."

"All the same," admitted Tutt, slightly wavering, "I see what Mr. Tutt means."

"Oh, I see what he means!" sniffed Miss Wiggin. "I was only combating what he said!"

"But the making of laws does not demonstrate progress," perversely insisted Mr. Tutt. "The more statutes you pass the more it indicates that you need 'em. An ideal community would have no laws at all."

"There's a thought!" interjected Tutt. "And there wouldn't be any lawyers either!"

"As King Hal said: 'The first thing we do, let's kill all the lawyers,'" commented Mr. Tutt.

"Awful vision!" ejaculated Miss Wiggin. "Luckily for us, that day has not yet dawned. However, Mr. Tutt's argument is blatantly fallacious. Of course, the making of new laws indicates an impulse toward social betterment—and therefore toward progress."

"It seems to me," ventured Tutt, "that this conversation is more than usually theoretical—not to say specious! The fact of the matter is that the law is a part of our civilization and the state of the law marks the stage of our development—more or less."

Mr. Tutt smiled sardonically.

"You have enunciated two great truths," said he. "First, that it is a 'part'; and second, 'more or less.' The law is a very small part of our protection against what is harmful to us. It is only one of our sanctions of conduct, and a very crude one at that. Did you ever stop to think that compared with religion the efficacy of the law was almost *nil*? The law deals with conduct, but only at a certain point. We are apt to find fault with it because it makes what appear to us to be arbitrary and unreasonable distinctions. That in large measure is because law is only supplementary."

"How do you mean—supplementary?" queried Tutt.

"Why," answered his partner, "as James C. Carter pointed out, ninety-nine per cent of all law is unwritten. What keeps most people straight is not criminal statutes but their own sense of decency, conscience or whatever you may choose to call it. Doubtless you recall the famous saying of Diogenes Laertius: 'There is a written and an unwritten law. The one by which we regulate our constitutions in our cities is the written law; that which arises from custom is the unwritten law.' I see that, of course you do! As I was saying only the other day, infractions of good taste and of manners, civil wrongs, sins, crimes—are in essence one and the same, differing only in degree. Thus the man who goes out to dinner without a collar violates the laws of social usage; if he takes all his clothes off and walks the streets he commits a crime. In a measure it simply depends on how many clothes he has on what grade of offense he commits. From that point of view the man who is not a gentleman is in a sense a criminal. But the law can't make a man a gentleman."

"I should say not!" murmured Miss Wiggin.

"Well," continued Mr. Tutt, "we have various ways of dealing with these outlaws. The man who violates our ideas of good taste or good manners is sent to Coventry; the man who does you a wrong is mulcted in damages; the sinner is held under the town pump and ridden out of town on a rail, or the church takes a hand and threatens him with the hereafter; but if he crosses a certain line we arrest him and lock him up—either from public spirit or for our own private ends."

"Hear! Hear!" cried Tutt admiringly.

"Fundamentally there is only an arbitrary distinction between wrongs, sins and crimes. The meanest and most detestable of men, beside whom an honest burglar is a sympathetic human being, may yet never violate a criminal statute."

"That's so!" said Tutt. "Take Badger, for instance."

"How often we defend cases," ruminated his partner, "where the complainant is just as bad as the prisoner at the bar—if not worse."

"And of course," added Tutt, "you must admit there are a lot of criminals who are criminals from perfectly good motives. Take the man, for instance, who thrashes a bystander who insults his wife—the man's wife, I mean, naturally."

"Only in those cases where we elect to take the law into our own hands we ought to be willing to accept the consequences like gentlemen and sportsmen," commented the senior partner.

"This is all very interesting, no doubt," remarked Miss Wiggin, "but as a matter of general information I should like to know why the criminal law doesn't punish the sinners—as well as the criminals."

"I guess one reason," replied Tutt, "is that people don't wish to be kept from sinning."

"Thou hast spoken!" agreed Mr. Tutt. "And another reason is that the criminal law was not originally devised for the purpose of eradicating sin—which, after all, is the state into which it is said man was born—but was only intended to prevent certain kinds of physical violence and lawlessness—murder, highway robbery, assault, and so on. The church was supposed to take care of sin, and there was an elaborate system of ecclesiastical courts. In point of fact, though there is a great deal of misconception on the subject, the criminal law does not deal with sin as sin at all, or even with wrongs merely as wrongs. It has a precise and limited purpose—namely, to prevent certain kinds of acts and to compel the performance of other acts.

"The state relies on the good taste and sense of decency, duty and justice of the individual citizen to keep him in order most of the time. It doesn't, or anyhow it shouldn't, attempt to deal with trifling peccadillos; it generally couldn't. It merely says that if a man's conscience and idea of fair play aren't enough to make him behave himself, why, then, when he gets too obstreperous we'll lock him up. And different generations have had entirely different ideas about what was too obstreperous to be overlooked. In the early days the law only punished bloodshed and violence. Later on, its scope was increased, until thousands of acts and omissions are now made criminal by statute. But that explains why the fact that something is a sin doesn't necessarily mean that it is a crime. The law is artificial and not founded on any general attempt to prohibit what is unethical, but simply to prevent what is immediately dangerous to life, limb and property."

"Which, after all, is a good thing—for it leaves us free to do as we choose so long as we don't harm anybody else," said Miss Wiggin.

"Yet," her employer continued, "unfortunately—or perhaps fortunately from our professional point of view—our lawmakers from time to time get rather hysterical and pass such a multiplicity of statutes that nobody knows whether he is committing crime or not."

"In this enlightened state," interposed Tutt, "it's a crime to advertise as a divorce lawyer; to attach a corpse for payment of debt; to board a train while it is in motion; to plant oysters without permission; or without authority wear the badge of the Patrons of Husbandry."

"Really, one would have to be a student to avoid becoming a criminal," commented Miss Wiggin.

Mr. Tutt rose and, looking along one of the shelves, took down a volume which he opened at a point marked by a burned match thrust between the leaves.

"My old friend Joseph H. Choate," he remarked, "in his memorial of his partner, Charles H. Southmayde, who was generally regarded as one of the greatest lawyers of our own or any other generation, says, 'The ever-growing list of misdemeanors, created by statute, disturbed him, and he even employed counsel to watch for such statutes introduced into the legislature—mantraps, as he called them—lest he might, without knowing it, commit offenses which might involve the penalty of imprisonment.'"

"We certainly riot in the printed word," said Miss Wiggin. "Do you know that last year alone to interpret all those statutes and decide the respective rights of our citizens the Supreme Court of this state wrote five thousand eight hundred pages of opinion?"

"Good Lord!" ejaculated Tutt. "Is that really so?"

"Of course it is!" she answered.

"But who reads the stuff?" demanded the junior partner. "I don't!"

"The real lawyers," replied Miss Wiggin innocently.

"The judges who write them probably read them," declared Mr. Tutt. "And the defeated litigants; the successful ones merely read the final paragraphs."

"But coming back to crime for a moment," said Miss Wiggin, pouring herself out a second cup of tea; "I had almost forgotten that the criminal law was originally intended only to keep down violence. That explains a lot of things. I confess to being one of those who unconsciously assumed that the law is a sort of official Mrs. Grundy."

"Not at all! Not at all!" corrected Mr. Tutt. "The law makes no pretense of being an arbiter of morals. Even where justice is concerned it expects the mere sentiment of the community to be capable of dealing with trifling offenses. The laws of etiquette and manners, devised for 'the purpose of keeping fools at a distance,' are reasonably adapted to enforcing the dictates of good taste and to dealing with minor offenses against our ideas of propriety."

"I wonder," hazarded Miss Wiggin thoughtfully, "if there isn't some sociological law about crimes, like the law of diminishing returns in physics?"

"The law of what?"

"Why, the law that the greater the force or effort applied to anything," she explained a little vaguely, "the greater the resistance becomes, until the effort doesn't accomplish anything; increased speed in a warship, for instance."

"What's that got to do with crime?"

"Why, the more statutes you pass and more new crimes you create the harder it becomes to enforce obedience to them, until finally you can't enforce them at all."

"That is rather a profound analogy," observed Mr. Tutt. "It might well repay study."

"Miss Wiggin has no corner on analogies," chirped Tutt. "Passing statutes creating new crimes is like printing paper money without anything back of it; in the one case there isn't really any more money than there was before and in the other there isn't really any more crime either."

"Only it makes more business for us."

"I've got another idea," continued Tutt airily, "and that is that crime is a good thing. Not because it means progress or any bunk like that, but because unless you had a certain amount of crime, and also criminal lawyers to attack the law, the state would never find out the weaknesses in its statutes. Therefore the more crime there is the more the protective power of the state is built up, just as the fever engendered by vaccine renders the human body immune from smallpox! Eh, what?"

"I never heard such nonsense!" exclaimed Miss Wiggin. "Do let me give you some more tea! Eh, what?"

But at that moment Willie announced that Mr. Rutherford Wells was calling to see Mr. Tutt and tea was hastily adjourned. Half an hour later the old lawyer rang for Bonnie Doon.

"Bonnie," he said, "one of our clients has been complained against by her next-door neighbor, a got-rich-quick lady, for obstructing the street with her motor. It's obviously a case of social envy, hatred and malice. Just take a run up there in the morning, give Mrs. Pierpont Pumpelly and her premises the once-over and let me know of any violations you happen to observe. I don't care how technical they are, either."

"All right, Mr. Tutt," answered Bonnie. "I get you. Isn't there a new ordinance governing the filling of garbage cans?"

"I think there is," nodded Mr. Tutt. "And meantime I think I'll drop over and see Judge O'Hare."

"I'll settle her hash for her, the hussy!" declared Mrs. Pumpelly to her husband at dinner the following evening. "I'll teach her to insult decent people and violate the law. Just because her husband belongs to a swell club she thinks she can do as she likes! But I'll show her! Wait till I get her in court to-morrow!"

"Well, of course, Edna, I'll stand back of you and all that," Pierpont assured her. "No, thank you, Simmons, I don't wish any more 'voly vong.' But I'd hate to see you get all messed up in a police court!"

"Me—messed up!" she exclaimed haughtily. "I guess I can take care of myself most anywheres—good and plenty!"

"Of course you can, dearie!" he protested in a soothing tone. "But these shyster lawyers who hang around those places—you 'member Jim O'Leary out home to Athens? Well, they don't know a lady when they see one, and they wouldn't care if they did; and they'll try and pry into your past life—"

"I haven't got any past life, and you know it too, Pierpont Pumpelly!" she retorted hotly. "I'm a respectable, law-abidin' woman, I am. I never broke a law in all my days—"

"Excuse me, madam," interposed Simmons, with whom the second footman had just held a whispered conference behind the screen, "but James informs me that there is a police hofficer awaiting to see you in the front 'all."

"To see me?" ejaculated Mrs. Pumpelly.

"Yes, madam."

"I suppose it's about to-morrow. Tell him to call round about nine o'clock in the morning."

"'E says 'e must see you to-night, ma'am," annotated James excitedly. "And 'e acted most hobnoxious to me!"

"Oh, he acted obnoxious, did he?" remarked Mrs. Pumpelly airily. "What was he obnoxious about?"

"'E 'as a paper 'e says 'e wants to serve on you personal," answered James in agitation. "'E says if you will hallow 'm to step into the dining-room 'e won't take a minute."

"Perhaps we'd better let him come in," mildly suggested Pierpont. "It's always best to keep on good terms with the police."

"But I haven't broken any law," repeated Mrs. Pumpelly blankly.

"Maybe you have without knowin' it," commented her husband.

"Why, Pierpont Pumpelly, you know I never did such a thing!" she retorted.

"Well, let's have him in, anyway," he urged. "I can't digest my food with him sitting out there in the hall."

Mrs. Pumpelly took control of the situation.

"Have the man in, Simmons!" she directed grandly.

And thereupon entered Officer Patrick Roony. Politely Officer Roony removed his cap, politely he unbuttoned several yards of blue overcoat and fumbled in the caverns beneath. Eventually he brought forth a square sheet of paper—it had a certain familiarity of aspect for Mrs. Pumpelly—and handed it to her.

"Sorry to disturb you, ma'am," he apologized, "but I was instructed to make sure and serve you personal."

"That's all right! That's all right!" said Pierpont with an effort at bonhomie. "The—er—butler will give you a highball if you say so."

"Oh, boy, lead me to it!" murmured Roony in the most approved manner of East Fourteenth Street. "Which way?"

"Come with me!" intoned Simmons with the exalted gesture of an archbishop conducting an ecclesiastical ceremonial.

"What does it say?" asked her husband hurriedly as the butler led the cop to it.

"Sh-h!" warned Mrs. Pumpelly. "James, kindly retire!"

James retired, and the lady examined the paper by the tempered light of the shaded candles surrounding what was left of the "voly vong."

"Who ever heard of such a thing?" she cried. "Just listen here, Pierpont!"

"CITY MAGISTRATE'S COURT, CITY OF NEW YORK

"In the name of the people of the State of New York

"To 'Maggie' Pumpelly, the name 'Maggie' being fictitious:

"You are hereby summoned to appear before the ———— District Magistrate's Court, Borough of Manhattan, City of New York, on the tenth day of May, 1920, at ten o'clock in the forenoon, to answer to the charge made against you by William Mulcahy for violation of Section One, Article Two, of the Police Traffic Regulations in that on May 7, 1920, you permitted a vehicle owned or controlled by you to stop with its left side to the curb on a street other than a one-way traffic street; and also for violation of Section Seventeen, Article Two of Chapter Twenty-four of the Code of Ordinances of the City of New York in that on the date aforesaid, being the owner of a vehicle subject to Subdivision One of said section and riding therein, you caused or permitted the same to proceed at a rate of speed greater than four miles an hour in turning corner of intersecting highways, to wit, Park Avenue and Seventy-third Street; and upon your failure to appear at the time and place herein mentioned you are liable to a fine of not exceeding fifty dollars or to imprisonment of not exceeding ten days or both.

"Dated 7th day of May, 1920.

"PATRICK ROONY, Police Officer,

"Police Precinct ———,

"New York City.

"Attest: JOHN J. JONES,

"Chief City Magistrate."

"Well, I never!" she exploded. "What rubbish! Four miles an hour! And 'Maggie'—as if everybody didn't know my name was Edna!"

"The whole thing looks a bit phony to me!" muttered Pierpont, worried over the possibility of having wasted a slug of the real thing on an unreal police officer. "Perhaps that feller wasn't a cop at all!"

"And who's William Mul-kay-hay?" she continued. "I don't know any such person! You better call up Mr. Edgerton right away and see what the law is."

"I hope he knows!" countered Mr. Pumpelly. "Four miles an hour—that's a joke! A baby carriage goes faster than four miles an hour. You wouldn't arrest a baby!"

"Well, call him up!" directed Mrs. Pumpelly. "Tell him he should come right round over here."

The summons from his client interrupted Mr. Edgerton in the middle of an expensive dinner at his club and he left it in no good humor. He didn't like being ordered round like a servant the way Mrs. Pumpelly was ordering him. It wasn't dignified. Moreover, a lawyer out of his office was like a snail out of its shell—at a distinct disadvantage. You couldn't just make an excuse to step into the next office for a moment and ask somebody what the law was. The Edgertons always kept somebody in an adjoining office who knew the law—many lawyers do.

On the Pumpelly stoop the attorney found standing an evil-looking and very shabby person holding a paper in his hand, but he ignored him until the grilled iron *cinquecento* door swung open, revealing James, the retiring second man.

Then, before he could enter, the shabby person pushed past him and asked in a loud, vulgar tone: "Does Edna Pumpelly live here?"

James stiffened in the approved style of erect vertebrata.

"This is Madame Pierpont Pumpelly's residence," he replied with hauteur.

"Madam or no madam, just slip this to her," said the shabby one. "Happy days!"

Mr. Wilfred Edgerton beneath the medieval tapestry of the Pumpelly marble hall glanced at the dirty sheet in James' hand and, though unfamiliar with the form of the document, perceived it to be a summons issued on the application of one Henry J. Goldsmith and returnable next day, for violating Section Two Hundred and Fifteen of Article Twelve of Chapter Twenty of the Municipal Ordinances for keeping and maintaining a certain bird, to wit, a cockatoo, which by its noise did disturb the quiet and repose of a certain person in the vicinity to the detriment of the health of such person, to wit, Henry J. Goldsmith, aforesaid, and upon her failure to appear, and so on.

Wilfred had some sort of vague idea of a law about keeping birds, but he couldn't exactly recall what it was. There was something incongruous about Mrs. Pierpont Pumpelly keeping a cockatoo. What did anybody want of a cockatoo? He concluded that it must be an ancestral hereditament from Athens, Ohio. Nervously he ascended the stairs to what Edna called the saloon.

"So you've come at last!" cried she. "Well, what have you got to say to this? Is it against the law to go round a corner at more than four miles an hour?"

Now, whereas Mr. Wilfred Edgerton could have told Mrs. Pumpelly the "rule in Shelly's case" or explained the doctrine of *cy pres*, he had never read the building code or the health ordinances or the traffic regulations, and in the present instance the latter were to the point while the former were not. Thus he was confronted with the disagreeable alternative of admitting his ignorance or bluffing it through. He chose the latter, unwisely.

"Of course not! Utter nonsense!" replied he blithely. "The lawful rate of speed is at least fifteen miles an hour."

"Excuse me, madam," said James, appearing once more in the doorway. "A man has just left this—er—paper at the area doorway."

Mrs. Pumpelly snatched it out of his hand.

"Well, of all things!" she gasped.

"To 'Bridget' Pumpelly," it began, "said first name 'Bridget' being fictitious: "You are hereby summoned to appear ... for violating Section Two Hundred and Forty-eight of Article Twelve of Chapter Twenty of the Health Ordinances in that you did upon the seventh day of May, 1920, fail to keep a certain tin receptacle used for swill or garbage, in shape and form a barrel, within the building occupied and owned by you until proper time for its removal and failed to securely bundle, tie up and pack the newspapers and other light refuse and rubbish contained therein, and, further, that you caused and permitted certain tin receptacles, in the shape and form of barrels, containing such swill or garbage, to be filled to a greater height with such swill or garbage than a line within such receptacle four inches from the top thereof."

"Now what do you know about that?" remarked the vice president of Cuban Crucible to the senior partner of Edgerton & Edgerton.

"I don't know anything about it!" answered the elegant Wilfred miserably. "I don't know the law of garbage, and there's no use pretending that I do. You'd better get a garbage lawyer."

"I thought all lawyers were supposed to know the law!" sniffed Mrs. Pumpelly. "What's that you got in your hand?"

"It's another summons, for keeping a bird," answered the attorney.

"A bird? You don't suppose it's Moses?" she exclaimed indignantly.

"The name of the bird isn't mentioned," said Wilfred. "But very likely it is Moses if Moses belongs to you."

"But I've had Moses ever since I was a little girl!" she protested. "And no one ever complained of him before."

"Beg pardon, madam," interposed Simmons, parting the Flemish arras, upon which was depicted the sinking of the Spanish Armada. "Officer Roony is back again with two more papers. 'E says it isn't necessary for him to see you again, as once is enough, but 'e was wondering whether being as it was rather chilly—"

"Lead him to it!" hastily directed Pierpont, who was beginning to get a certain amount of enjoyment out of the situation. "But tell him he needn't call again."

"Give 'em here!" snapped Mrs. Pumpelly, grasping the documents. "This is a little too much! 'Lulu' this time. Fictitious as usual. Who's Julius Aberthaw? He says I caused a certain rug to be shaken in such place and manner that certain particles of dust passed therefrom into the public street or highway, to wit, East Seventy-third Street, contrary to

"What's the other one?" inquired her husband with a show of sympathy.

"For violating Section Fifteen of Article Two of Chapter Twenty, in that on May 7, 1920, I permitted a certain unmuzzled dog, to wit, a Pekingese brown spaniel dog, to be on a public highway, to wit, East Seventy-third Street in the City of New York. But that was Randolph!"

"Was Randolph muzzled?" inquired Mr. Edgerton maliciously.

"Of course not! He only weighs two pounds and a quarter!" protested Mrs. Pumpelly.

"He can bite all right, just the same!" interpolated Pierpont.

"But what shall I do?" wailed Mrs. Pumpelly, now thoroughly upset.

"Guess you'll have to take your medicine, same's other violators of the law," commented her husband.

"I never heard of such ridiculous laws!"

"Ignorance of the law excuses no one!" murmured Wilfred.

"It don't excuse a lawyer!" she snorted. "I have an idea you don't know much more about the law—this kind of law, anyway—than I do. I bet it is against the law to go round a corner at more than four miles! Do you want to bet me?"

"No, I don't!" snapped Edgerton. "What you want is a police-court lawyer—if you're goin' in for this sort of thing."

"My Lord! What's this now, Simmons?" she raved as the butler deprecatingly made his appearance again with another paper.

"I think, madam," he answered soothingly, "that it's a summons for allowing the house man to use the hose on the sidewalk after eight A.M. Roony just brought it."

"H'm!" remarked Mr. Pumpelly. "Don't lead him to it again!"

"But I wouldn't have disturbed you if it hadn't been for a young gentleman who 'as called with another one regardin' the window boxes."

"What about window boxes?" moaned Mrs. Pumpelly.

"'E says," explained Simmons, "'e 'as a summons for you regardin' the window boxes, but that if you'd care to speak to him perhaps the matter might be adjusted—"

"Let's see the summons!" exclaimed Wilfred, coming to life.

"'To Edna Pumpelly,'" he read.

"They're gettin' more polite," she commented ironically.

"'For violating Section Two Hundred and Fifty of Article Eighteen of Chapter Twenty-three in that you did place, keep and maintain upon a certain window sill of the premises now being occupied by you in the City of New York a window box for the cultivation or retention of flowers, shrubs, vines or other articles or things without the same being firmly protected by iron railings—'"

"Heavens," ejaculated Mr. Pumpelly, "there'll be somebody here in a minute complaining that I don't use the right length of shaving stick."

"I understand," remarked Mr. Edgerton, "that in a certain Western state they regulate the length of bed sheets!"

"What's that for?" asked Edna with sudden interest.

"About seeing this feller?" hurriedly continued Mr. Pumpelly. "Seems to me they've rather got you, Edna!"

"But what's the use seein' him?" she asked. "I'm summoned, ain't I?"

"Why not see the man?" advised Mr. Edgerton, gladly seizing this possibility of a diversion. "It cannot do any harm."

"What is his name?"

"Mr. Bonright Doon," answered Simmons encouragingly. "And he is a very pleasant-spoken young man."

"Very well," yielded Mrs. Pumpelly.

Two minutes later, "Mr. Doon!" announced Simmons.

Though the friends of Tutt & Tutt have made the acquaintance of Bonnie Doon only casually, they yet have seen enough of him to realize that he is an up-and-coming sort of young person with an elastic conscience and an ingratiating smile. Indeed the Pumpellys were rather taken with his breezy "Well, here we all are again!" manner as well as impressed by the fact that he was arrayed in immaculate evening costume.

"I represent Mr. Ephraim Tutt, who has been retained by your neighbor, Mrs. Rutherford Wells, in connection with the summons which you caused to be issued against her yesterday," he announced pleasantly by way of introduction. "Mrs. Wells, you see, was a little annoyed by being referred to in the papers as Jane when her proper name is Beatrix. Besides, she felt that the offense charged against her was—so to speak—rather trifling. However—be that as it may—she and her friends in the block are not inclined to be severe with you if you are disposed to let the matter drop."

"Inclined to be severe with me!" ejaculated Mrs. Pumpelly, bristling.

"Edna!" cautioned her husband. "Mr. Doon is not responsible."

"Exactly. I find after a somewhat casual investigation that you have been consistently violating a large number of city ordinances—keeping parrots, beating rugs, allowing unmuzzled dogs at large, overfilling your garbage cans, disregarding the speed laws and traffic regulations, using improperly secured window boxes—"

"Anything else?" inquired Pierpont jocularly. "Don't mind us."

Bonnie carelessly removed from the pocket of his dress coat a sheaf of papers.

"One for neglecting to have your chauffeur display his metal badge on the outside of his coat—Section Ninety-four of Article Eight of Chapter Fourteen.

"One for allowing your drop awnings to extend more than six feet from the house line—Section Forty-two of Article Five of Chapter Twenty-two.

"One for failing to keep your curbstone at a proper level—Section One Hundred and Sixty-four of Article Fourteen of Chapter Twenty-three.

"One for maintaining an ornamental projection on your house—a statue, I believe, of the Goddess Venus—to project more than five feet beyond the building line—Section One Hundred and Eighty-one of Article Fifteen of Chapter Twenty-three.

"One for having your area gate open outwardly instead of inwardly—Section One Hundred and Sixty-four of Article Fourteen of Chapter Twenty-three.

"And one for failing to affix to the fanlight or door the street number of your house—Section One Hundred and Ten of Article Ten of Chapter Twenty-three.

"I dare say there are others."

"I'd trust you to find 'em!" agreed Mr. Pumpelly. "Now what's your proposition? What does it cost?"

"It doesn't cost anything at all! Drop your proceedings and we'll drop ours," answered Bonnie genially.

"What do you say, Edgerton?" said Pumpelly, turning to the disgruntled Wilfred and for the first time in years assuming charge of his own domestic affairs.

"I should say that it was an excellent compromise!" answered the lawyer soulfully. "There's something in the Bible, isn't there, about pulling the mote out of your own eye before attempting to remove the beam from anybody's else?"

"I believe there is," assented Bonnie politely. "'You're another' certainly isn't a statutory legal plea, but as a practical defense—"

"Tit for tat!" said Mr. Edgerton playfully. "Ha, ha! Ha!"

"Ha, ha! Ha!" mocked Mrs. Pumpelly, her nose high in air. "A lot of good you did me!"

"By the way, young man," asked Mr. Pumpelly, "whom do you say you represent?"

"Tutt & Tutt," cooed Bonnie, instantly flashing one of the firm's cards.

"Thanks," said Pumpelly, putting it carefully into his pocket. "I may need you sometime—perhaps even sooner. Now, if by any chance you'd care for a highball—"

"Lead me right to it!" sighed Bonnie ecstatically.

"Me, too!" echoed Wilfred, to the great astonishment of those assembled.

Beyond a Reasonable Doubt

"For twelve honest men have decided the cause,
Who are judges alike of the fact and the laws."
—The Honest Jury.

"Lastly," says Stevenson in his Letter to a Young Gentleman Who Proposes to Embrace the Career of Art, "we come to those vocations which are at once decisive and precise; to the men who are born with the love of pigments, the passion of drawing, the gift of music, or the impulse to create with words, just as other and perhaps the same men are born with the love of hunting, or the sea, or horses, or the turning lathe. These are predestined; if a man love the labor of any trade, apart from any question of success or fame, the gods have called him."

Had anybody told Danny Lowry that the gods had called him he would have stigmatized his informant as a liar—yet they had. For apart from any question of success or fame he had loved horses from the day when as a baby he had first sprawled in the straw of his Uncle Mike Aherne's livery and hitching stable in Dublin City. He had grown up to the scrape and whiffle of the currycomb, breathing ammonia, cracking the skin of his infantile knuckles with harness soap. Out of the love that he bore for the beautiful dumb brutes grew an understanding that in time became almost uncanny. All the jockeys and hostlers said there was magic in the lad's hands. He could ride anything on hoofs with a slack rein; and the worst biter in the stable would take a bridle from him as it were an apple.

"Oft, now, I hear him talkin' to 'em, so I do." Mike Aherne was wont to say between spits. "An' they know what he says, I'm tellin' ye. He's a charmer, he is; like the Whisperin' Blacksmith. You've heard tell of him, belike? Well, Danny can spake to 'em widout even a whisper, so he can that!"

That was near seventy years agone, and now Danny was a shrunken little white-haired old wastrel who haunted Mulqueen's Livery over on Twenty-fourth Street near Tenth Avenue, disappearing in and out of the cellar and loft and stalls like a leprechaun haunts a hollow tree. Nobody knew where he had come from or where he lived except that he could always be found wherever there was a suffering animal, be it dog, cat or squirrel, and the rest of the time at Mulqueen's, with whom he had an understanding about the telephone. He was short, wiry, unshaven, with the legs of a jockey; and when he could get it he drank. That, however, was not why he had left Ireland, which had had something to do with Phoenix Park; nor was it the cause of the decline of his fortunes, which had been the coming of the motor.

Some day a story must be written called The Hitching Post, about those thousands of little cast-iron negro boys who stand so patiently on the green grass strips along village streets waiting to hold long-forgotten bridle reins. They lost their usefulness a decade or more ago, and so, by the same token and at the same time, did all that army of people who lived and moved and had their being by ministering to the needs of the horse. The gas engine was to them what the mechanical bobbin was to the spinners of Liverpool and Belfast. With the coming of the motor the race of coachmen, grooms and veterinaries began to perish from the earth. Among the last was Danny Lowry, at the very zenith of his fortunes an unofficial vet to most of the swell stables belonging to the carriage people of Fifth Avenue. One by one these stables had been converted into garages, and the broughams and C-spring victorias, the landaus and basket phaetons had been dragged to the auction room or shoved into dim corners to make room for snappy motors; and the horses Danny knew and loved so well had been sold or turned out to grass.

But there was nobody to turn Danny out to grass. He had to keep going. So he had drifted lower and lower, passing from the private stable to the trucking stable, and from the trucking stable to the last remaining decrepit boarding and liveries of the remote West Side. The tragedy of the horse is the tragedy of all who loved them. Danny was one of these tragedies, but he still picked up a precarious living by doing odd jobs at Mulqueen's and acting as a veterinary when called upon, and he could generally be found either loafing in the smelly little office or smoking his T D pipe on the steps outside.

He and Mr. Ephraim Tutt, the lawyer, who lived in the rickety old house with the tall windows and piazzas protected by railings of open ironwork round which twisted the stems of extinct wistarias, had long been friends. Many a summer evening the two old men had sat together and discoursed of famous jockeys and still more famous horses, of Epsom and Ascot, until Mr. Tutt's cellaret was empty and never a stogy left in the box at all. Probably no one save the odd lanky old attorney, who himself seemed to belong to a bygone era, knew the story of Danny's glorious past—how he had risen from his Uncle Aherne's livery in Dublin first to being paddock groom to Lord Ashburnham and then to jockey, finally to ride the Derby under the Farringdon gold and crimson, and to carry away Katherine Brady, the second housemaid, as Mrs. Lowry when he went back to Dublin with a goodly pile of money to take over his uncle's business; and how thereafter had come babies, and fever, and the epizootic, and hard times; and Danny, a heartbroken man, had fled from bereavement and pauperism and possibly from prison to seek his fortune in America. And then the motor! Lastly, now, a hand-to-mouth, furtive, ignorant old age, a struggle for bare existence and to keep the tiny flat going for his seventeen-year-old granddaughter, Katie, who kept house for him and of whose existence few, even of Danny's friends, were aware excepting Mr. Tutt.

There was, in fact, a striking parallel between these two old men, the one so ignorant, the other so essentially a man of culture, in that they were both humanitarians in a high sense. It is improbable that Ephraim Tutt was conscious of what drew him to Danny Lowry, but drawn he was; and the reason for it was that the fundamental mainspring of the life of each was love—in the case of the man of law for those of his fellow men who suffered through foolishness or poverty or weaknesses or misfortune; and in that of his more humble counterpart, whose limitations precluded his understanding of more endowed human beings, for the dumb animals, who must mutely suffer through the foolishness or poverty or weakness or misfortune of their owners and masters.

Danny had sat up all night with only a horse blanket drawn over his legs, taking care of a roan mare with the croup. The helpless thing had lain flat on her side in the straw struggling for breath, and Danny, his heart racked with pity, had sat in the stall beside her, every hour giving her steam and gently pouring his own secret mixture down her throat. Nobody but Danny cared what became of the mare, left there two weeks before by a stranger who had not returned for it; stolen, probably. Cramped, stiff with rheumatism, half dead from fatigue and suffering from a bad cough himself, he left the stable at eight o'clock next morning, hopeful that the miserable beast would pull through, and stepped round to Salvatore's lunch cart for a bowl of coffee and a hot dog. He was just lighting his pipe preparatory to going back to the stable when a stranger pulled up to the curb in a mud-splashed depot wagon.

"'Morning," he remarked pleasantly. "Can you tell me if Mulqueen's livery stable is anywhere about here?"

Danny removed his pipe and spat politely.

"Sure," he replied, taking in the horse, which besides being lame and having a glaring spavin on its off hind leg was a mere bone bag fit only for the soap factory. "'Tis just forninst the corner. I'm after goin' there meself."

The stranger, a heavy-faced man with a thick neck, nodded.

"All right. You go along and I'll follow."

Mulqueen was not yet at the stable and Danny helped unharness the animal, which, as soon as relieved of the shafts, hung its head between its legs, evidently all in. The stranger handed Danny a cigar.

"I'm lookin' for a vet," said he. "My horse ought to have something done for him."

"I can well see that!" agreed Danny. "He needs a poultice and hot bandages. A bit of rest wouldn't do him no harm, neither."

"Well, I'm no vet," returned the stranger with an apologetic grin, "but it don't take much to know that he's a sick horse. I'm a doctor, myself, but not a horse doctor. Have you got one here?"

"Some calls me a horse doctor," modestly answered Danny. "I can treat a spavin and wind a bandage as well as the next. How long will you be leavin' him?"

"Oh, a day or two, I guess. Well, if you're a veterinary I leave him in your care. My name's Simon—Dr. Joseph R. Simon, of Hempstead, Long Island."

Danny worked all the morning over the horse, doing his best to make it comfortable. Indeed, before he had concluded his treatment the animal was probably more comfortable than he, for the night in the cold stall had given him a chill and when he left the stable to go home for lunch he was in a high fever. Doctor Simon was outside on the sidewalk talking to Mulqueen.

"Well, doctor," said he, "what did you find was the matter with my horse?"

"Spavin, lame in three legs, sore eyes, underfed," replied Danny, shivering. "Sure an' he's a sick animal."

"How much do I owe you?" inquired Doctor Simon.

Danny was about to answer that a couple of dollars would be all right when the thought occurred to him that here was an opportunity to secure medical treatment for himself.

"If you'll give me something to stop a fever we'll call it even," he suggested.

"That's easy!" returned Doctor Simon heartily. "Come into the office and I'll take your temperature and write you out a prescription."

So they sat down by the stove and the doctor took Danny's pulse and put a thermometer under his tongue, chatting amicably meanwhile, and when he had completed his examination he wrote something on a piece of paper.

"How long have you been practicing veterinary medicine?" he inquired.

"All my life," answered Danny truthfully. "But I don't get near so much to do as I used. These be hard times for those as have to do with horses."

He got up painfully.

"Well, now," said Doctor Simon, "I'd feel better if I paid you for treating my horse. Just put this five-dollar bill in your pocket. I guess you need it more than I do."

Danny shook his head. "That's all right!" he said weakly, for he was feeling very ill. "It's a stand-off."

"Oh, go ahead, take it!" urged Doctor Simon, shoving the bill into the pocket of Danny's overcoat. "By the way, have you got your card? I might be able to send a little business your way."

When his magic skill with horses was matter of common knowledge among the upper circle of Long Island grooms and coachmen Danny had had a few cards struck off by a friendly printer. A couple of fly-blown specimens still lingered in the drawer of Mulqueen's desk. Danny searched until he found one:

DANIEL LOWRY
VETERINARY

212 WEST 53D STREET
NEW YORK CITY

"Here, sor," said he, his head swimming, "that's my name, but the address is wrong."

Doctor Simon put it in his pocketbook.

"Thanks," he remarked. "Much obliged for fixing up my horse." Then in a businesslike manner, he threw back his coat and displayed a glittering badge. "Now," he added brusquely, "I must arrest you for practising veterinary medicine without a license. Just come along with me to the nearest police station."

When Mr. Tutt returned home that evening after attending one of the weekly sessions at the Colophon Club, where he had reluctantly contributed the sum of fifty-seven dollars to relieve the immediate needs of certain impecunious persons gathered there about a green-baize-covered table in a remote corner of the card room, he perceived by the light of an adjacent street lamp that someone was sitting upon the top of the steps leading to his front door.

"Are you Mr. Tutt?" inquired Katie Lowry, getting up and making a timid curtsy. "The great lawyer?"

"That is my name, child," he answered. "What do you want of me?"

She was but a wisp of a girl and her eyes shone like a cat's from under a gray shawl gathered over a pair of narrow, pinched shoulders.

"They've taken grandfather away to prison," she replied with a catch in her throat. "He didn't come in to lunch nor to supper, and when I went to the stable Mr. Mulqueen said a detective had arrested grandfather for doctoring horses without a license and he had pleaded guilty and they'd locked him up. I went to the police station, but they said he wasn't there any more, but that he was in the Tombs."

"Who is your grandfather?" demanded Mr. Tutt as he unlocked the door.

"Danny Lowry," she replied. "Oh, sir, won't you try to do something for him, sir? He thinks so much of you! He often has told me what a grand man you were and so kind, besides being such a clever lawyer and all the judges afraid of you!"

"Danny Lowry in the Tombs!" cried Mr. Tutt. "What an outrage! Of course I'll do what I can for him. But first come inside and warm yourself. Miranda!" he shouted to the colored maid of all work. "Make us some hot toast and tea and bring it up to the library. Now, my dear, take off your shawl and sit down and tell me all about it."

So with her frayed kid shoes upturned on the fender, little Katie Lowry, confident that she had found an all-powerful friend in this queer long man who smoked such queer long cigars, sipping her tea only when she had to pause for breath, poured out the story of her grandfather's fight with poverty and misfortune, while her auditor's wrinkled face grew soft and hard by turns as he watched her through the gray clouds from his stogy. An hour later he left her at the door of her flat, happy and encouraged, with a twenty-dollar bill crumpled in her hand.

By Advice of Counsel

"But what do you expect me to do about it?" retorted District Attorney Peckham in his office next morning when Mr. Tutt had explained to him the perversion of justice to accomplish which the law had been invoked. "I'm sorry! No doubt he's a good feller. But he's guilty, isn't he? Admitted it in the police court, didn't he?"

"I expect you to temper justice with mercy," replied Mr. Tutt earnestly. "This old man's whole life has been devoted to relieving the sufferings of animals. He's a genuine Samaritan."

"That's like saying that a thief has done good with his plunder, isn't it?" commented Peckham. "Look here, Tutt, of course I hope you get your man off and all that, but if I personally threw the case out I'd have all the vets in the city on my neck. You see the motors have pretty nearly put 'em all out of business. There aren't enough sick horses to go round, so they've been conducting a sort of crusade. Tough luck—but the law is the law. And I have to enforce it—ostensibly, anyway."

"Very well," answered the old lawyer amiably but defiantly. "Then if you've got to enforce the law against a fine old chap like that I've got to do my darnedest to smash that law higher than a kite. And I'll tell you something, Peckham—which is that the human heart is a damn sight bigger than the human conscience."

Danny Lowry had lived for years in fear of the blow which had so suddenly struck him down, for there had never been any blinking of the obvious fact that in acting as an unlicensed veterinary he was brazenly violating the law. On the other hand, not being able to read or write, and having no technical knowledge of medicine, all his experience, all his skill, all his love of animals could avail him nothing so far as securing a license was concerned. He could not read an examination paper, but he could interpret the symptoms seen in a trembling neck and a lack-luster eye. Danny had no choice but to break the law or abandon the only career for which he had an aptitude, or by which he could hope to earn a living at his age. His crime was *malum prohibitum*, not *malum in se*, but it was, nevertheless, a violation of a most necessary law. Certainly none of us wish to be doctored by tyros or humbugs, or to have our animals treated by them. Only Danny was neither a tyro nor a humbug, and had he not been a lawbreaker the world would have been to some extent the loser.

Yet by all the canons of ethics and justice it was most improper for Mr. Tutt to hurry off to the Tombs and bail out old Danny Lowry, a self-confessed lawbreaker, giving his own bond and the house on Twenty-third Street as security. Still more so, as more unblushingly ostentatious, was his taking the criminal over to Pont's and giving him the very best dinner that Signor Faccini, proprietor of that celebrated hostelry, could purvey.

Hard cases are said to make bad law; I wonder if they make bad people. If "conscience makes cowards of us all" does human sympathy play ducks and drakes with conscience? Does it blind the eye of reason? Rather, does it not illumine and expose the fallacies of logic and the falsities of the syllogism? Do two and two make four in human polity as in mathematics? Sometimes it would not seem so.

Certainly you would have picked Mr. Bently Gibson, of The Gibson Woolen Mills, as a model juror. One look at him as a prospective talesman in a murder case and you would have unhesitatingly murmured, "The defense challenges peremptorily!" His broad forehead, large well-shaped nose, firm chin and clear calm eye evidenced his common sense, his conscientiousness and his uncompromising adherence to principle. His customs declarations were complete to the smallest item, his income-tax returns models of self-sacrifice, he was patriotic and civic, he belonged to the Welfare League and the Citizens' Union, and—I hesitate to confess it—he subscribed to the annual deficit of the Society for the Suppression of Sin. On the face of it, he was the kind of man the district attorney tries to select as foreman of a jury when he has to prosecute a woman who had kidnaped her own child out of a foundling asylum.

The heelers and hangers-on of the criminal courts would have described him as a highbrow and as a holier-than-thou; perhaps he might in a moment of jocularity have even so described himself—for he had his human—perhaps I should have said, his weaker—side. Surely he seemed human enough when he kissed Eleanor good-by at the door of their country place on the Sound the morning he had been subpoenaed to serve as a juryman in Part Five of the General Sessions. He had planned to take a week's holiday that spring, and he had gone to infinite trouble to arrange his business in order to have it, for they had become engaged eleven years before at the moment when the apple blossoms and the dogwoods were at the height of their glory, even as they were now.

When, however, he found the brown subpoena at his office directing him to present himself for service the following Monday he simply gave a half sigh, half grunt of disgust, and let the longed-for vacation go; for one of his pet theories was that the jury system was the chief bulwark of the Constitution, the cornerstone of liberty. Had he only been disingenuous enough he need never have served on any jury, for no lawyer for the defense hearing him enlarge on what he considered the duties of a juryman to be, would ever have allowed him in the box. But when other chaps on the panel presented their excuses to the judge and managed to persuade him of the imperative needs of family or business, and slipped—grinning discreetly—out of the court room, he merely inaudibly called them welshers and pikers. No, he regarded jury service as a duty and a privilege, one not to be lightly avoided—the one common garden governmental function in which Uncle Sam expected every citizen to do his duty.

"I won't let any of the rogues get by me!" he shouted gaily to his wife over the back of the motor. "And anyhow I shan't be locked up all night. There aren't any murder cases on the calendar. I'll be out on the five-fifteen as usual."

Alas, poor Bently! Alas for human frailty and all those splendid visions in which he pictured himself as the anchor of the ship of justice, a prop and stay of the structure of democracy.

By Advice of Counsel

His train was a trifle late and the roll of the jury had already been called, and the perennial excuses heard, when he entered the court room; but the clerk, who knew him, nodded in a welcoming manner, checked him off as present and dropped his name card in the revolving wheel. It was a well-known scene to Bently, a veteran of fifteen years' service. Even the actors were familiar friends—the pink-faced judge with his snow-white whiskers, who at times suggested to Bently an octogenarian angel, and, at others, a certain ancient baboon once observed in the Primates cage at the Bronz Zoo; the harried, anxious little clerk with his paradoxically grandiloquent intonation; the comedy assistant district attorney with his wheezy voice emanating from a Falstaffian body, who suffered from a soporific malady and was accustomed to open a case and then let it take care of itself while he slumbered audibly beneath the dais; even Ephraim Tutt, the gaunt, benignly whimsical-looking attorney, in his rusty-black frock coat and loose-hanging tie; his rotund partner, whose birdlike briskness and fat paunch inevitably brought to mind a distended robin in specs; and the *dégagé* Bonnie Doon in his cut-in-at-the-waist checked suit—he knew them all of old.

"Well, call your first case, Mister District Attorney!" directed the judge, nodding encouragingly at Bently, well knowing that in him he had a staunch upholder of the law-as-it-is, who could be depended upon to bolster up his weaker or more sentimental brother talesmen into the proper convicting attitude of mind.

Then—as per the schedule in force for at least an epoch—good-natured, pot-bellied Tom Hingman, the oldest A.D.A. in the office, rose heavily, fumbled with his stubby fingers among the blue indictments on the table, drew one forth, panted a few times, gasped out "People against Daniel Lowry," and looked round in a pseudo-helpless way as if not knowing exactly what to do.

There was a slight stir, and from the back of the court room came forward a funny little bow-legged old man, carrying in both hands a funny little flat-topped derby hat, and took his seat timidly at the bar of justice beside Mr. Tutt, who smiled down at him affectionately and put his arm about the threadbare shoulders as if to protect him from the evils of the world. They made a quaint and far from unpleasing picture, thought Bently Gibson, the ideal juror, and he wondered what the poor old devil could be up for.

A jury was impaneled, Bently among them; the balance of the panel was excused until two o'clock; the court room was cleared of loafers; the judge perused the indictment with a practised eye; Tom Hingman rose again, wheezed and grinned at the embattled jury; and the mill of justice began to grind.

Now the mill of justice, at least in the General Sessions of New York County, grinds exceeding fine, so far as the number of convictions is concerned. Of those brought to the bar for trial few escape; for modern talesmen, being hard-headed men, regard the whole thing as a matter of business and try to get through with it as quickly and as efficiently as possible. The bombastic spread-eagle orator, the grandiloquent gas bag, the highfaluting stump speaker gain few verdicts and win small applause except from their clients. And district attorneys who ape the bloodhound in their mien and tactics win scant approval and less acquiescence from the bored gentlemen who are forced to listen to them. Nowadays—whatever may have been the case two generations ago—each side briefly states its claims and tries to win on points.

People were apt to wonder why each succeeding administration inevitably retained stuffy old Tom Hingman at seventy-five hundred dollars a year to handle the calendar in Part Five. Yet those on the inside knew why very well. It was because Tom long ago, in his prehistoric youth, had learned that the way to secure verdicts was to appear not to care a tinker's dam whether the jury found the defendant guilty or not. He pretended never to know anything about any case in advance, to be in complete ignorance as to who the witnesses might be and to what they were going to testify, and to be terribly sorry to have to prosecute the unfortunate at the bar, though he wasn't to blame for that any more than the jury were for having to find him guilty if proven to be so, which, it seemed to him, he had been clearly proven to be. I say Tom pretended all this, yet it was more than half true, for Tom was a kind-hearted old bird. But the point was that, whether true or not, it got convictions. The jury sucking it all up in its entirety felt sorrier for the simple-minded old softy of a Tom, which they believed him to be, than they did for the defendant, who they concluded was a good deal cleverer than the assistant district attorney.

In a word, it put them on their honor as public officers not to let the administration of justice suffer merely because the A.D.A. was too old and easy-going and generally slab-sided to be really on his job. Thus, they became prosecuting attorneys themselves—in all, thirteen to one. So Tom, having thus delegated his functions to the jury, calmly left it all to them and went to sleep, which was the best thing that he did. Worth seventy-five hundred a year? Rather, seventy-five thousand!

"Gentlemen of the jury," he began haltingly, "this defendant seems to have been indicted for the crime of practising medicine without a license—a misdemeanor. I don't see exactly how he gets into this court, which is supposed to try only felony cases, but I assume my old friend Tutt made a motion to transfer the case from the Special to the General Sessions on the theory that he would stand more chance with a jury than three—er—hardened judges. Well, maybe he will—I don't know! I gather from the papers that Mr. Lowry here, after holding himself out to be a properly licensed veterinary, treated a horse belonging to the complainant. It is not a very serious offense, and you and I have no great interest in the case, but of course the public has got to be protected from charlatans, and the only way to do it is to brand as guilty those who pretend they are duly licensed to practise medicine when they are not. If you had a sick baby, Mr. Foreman, and you saw a sign 'A.S. Smith, M.D., Children's Specialist,' you would want to be sure you were not going to hire a plumber, eh? You see! That's all there is to this case!"

"All there is to this case!" murmured Mr. Tutt audibly, raising his eyes ceilingward.

"Step up here, Mr. Brown."

Mr. Brown, the supposed Doctor Simon whose horse Danny had attended, seated himself complacently in the witness chair and bowed to the jury in a professional manner. He had, he told them, been a detective employed by the state board of health for over sixteen years. It was his duty to go round and arrest people who pretended to be licensed practitioners of medicine and assumed to doctor other people and animals. There were a lot of 'em, too; the jury would be surprised—

Mr. Tutt objected to their surprise and it was stricken out by order of the court.

"I'll strike out 'and there are a lot of 'em, too,' if you say so, Mr. Tutt," offered the court, smiling, but Mr. Tutt shook his head.

"No; let it stand!" said he significantly. "Let it stand!"

"Well, anyway," continued Mr. Brown, "this here defendant Lowry, as he calls himself, is well known—"

Objected to and struck out.

"Well, this here defendant makes a practise—"

"Strike it out! What did he do?" snapped the octogenarian baboon on the bench.

"I'm tellin' you, judge," protested Brown vigorously. "This here defendant—"

"You've said that three times!" retorted the baboon. "Get along, can't you? What did he do?"

"He treated my horse for spavin here in New York at 500 West 24th Street at my request on the twentieth of last March and I paid him five dollars. He said he was a licensed veterinary and he gave me his card. Here it is."

"Well, why didn't you say so before?" remarked the judge more amiably. "Let me see the card. All right! Anything more, Mr. Hingman?"

But Mr. Hingman had long before this subsided into his chair and was emitting sounds like those from a saxophone.

"That is plain, simple testimony, Mr. Tutt," remarked the judge. "Go ahead and cross-examine."

Ephraim Tutt slowly unjointed himself, the quintessence of affability, though Mr. Brown clearly held him under suspicion.

"How long have you earned your living, my dear sir, by going round arresting people?"

"Sixteen years."

"Under what name—your own?"

"I use any name I feel like."

Mr. Tutt nodded appreciatively.

"Let us see, then. You go about pretending to be somebody you are not?"

"Put it that way, if you choose."

"And pretending to be what you are not?"

Mr. Brown eyed Mr. Tutt savagely. "What do you mean by that?"

"Didn't you tell this old gentleman beside me that you were a doctor of medicine but not a doctor of veterinary medicine—and beg him to treat your horse for that reason?"

"Sure I did. Certainly."

"Well, are you a licensed medical practitioner?"

"Look here! What's that got to do with it?" snarled Mr. Brown, looking about for aid from the sleeping Hingman.

124

"The question is a proper one. Answer it," directed the judge.
"No, I'm not a licensed doctor."
"Well, didn't you treat Mr. Lowry?"
The jury by this time had caught the drift of the examination and were listening with intent appreciation.

Mr. Brown leaned forward, a sickening smile of sneering superiority curling about his yellow molars.

"Ah!" he cried. "That's where I have you, sir! I only pretended to treat him. I didn't really. I only scribbled something on a piece of paper."

"You knew he couldn't read, of course?"

"Sure."

Mr. Tutt turned to the uplifted faces of the twelve. "So," he retorted, pursing his wrinkled lips and placing his fingers together in that attitude of piety which we frequently observe upon effigies of defunct ecclesiastics—"so you did the very thing for which you threw this old man at my side into jail—and for which he is now on trial! You lied to him about being a doctor! You deceived him about giving him the medical treatment he so much needed! And you arrested him after he had worked for hours to relieve the sufferings of a sick animal. By the way, it was a sick animal, wasn't it?"

"The sickest I could find," replied Brown airily.

"And he did relieve its sufferings, did he not?" continued Mr. Tutt gently.

"Very likely. I wasn't particularly interested in that end of it."

Mr. Tutt's meager frame seemed suddenly to expand until he hung over the witness chair like the genii who mushroomed so unexpectedly out of the fisherman's bottle in the Arabian Nights Entertainments.

"You were not interested in ministering to a poor horse, so sick it could hardly stand! You were only interested in imprisoning and depriving of his only form of livelihood this old man whose heart was not hardened like yours! May I ask at whose instance you went and lied to him?"

"Mr. Tutt! Mr. Tutt!" interjected the octogenarian angel. "Your examination is exceeding the bounds of judicial propriety."

Ephraim Tutt bowed low.

"A thousand pardons, Your Honor! My emotions swept me away! I most humbly apologize! But when this witness so unblushingly confesses how he played the scoundrel's part, aged case hardened practitioner as I am, my heart cries out against such infamous treachery—"

Bang! went the judge's gavel.

"You are only making it worse!" declared the court severely. "Proceed with your examination."

"Very well, Your Honor!" replied Mr. Tutt, his lips trembling with well-simulated indignation. "Now, sir, who instigated this miserable deception—I beg Your Honor's pardon! Who put you up to this game—I mean, this course of conduct?"

"Nobody," replied Brown in a surly tone.

"Did you ever hear of the United Association of Veterinaries of the Greater City of New York—sometimes referred to as The Horse Leeches' Union?" asked Mr. Tutt insinuatingly.

Mr. Brown hesitated.

"I've heard of some such organization," he admitted. "But I never heard it was called a Horse Leeches' Union."

"Didn't one of its officers come to you and say that unless something was done to reduce competition they'd have to go out of business—owing to the decrease in horses in New York?"

"I don't remember," answered Brown slowly. "One of 'em may have said something of the sort to me. But that's my business!"

"Yes!" roared Mr. Tutt suddenly. "It's your business to pretend you're a doctor when you're not, and you walk the streets a free man; and you want to send my client to Sing Sing for the same offense! That is all! I am done with you! Get down off the stand! Do not let me detain you from the practise of your unlicensed profession!"

"Mr. Tutt!" again admonished His Honor as the lawyer threw himself angrily into his chair. "This really won't do at all!"

"I beg Your Honor's pardon—a thousand times!" said Mr. Tutt in tones so humble and sincere that he almost made the angel-faced baboon believe him.

I should like to go on and describe the whole course of Danny Lowry's trial item by item, witness by witness, and tell what Mr. Tutt did to each. But I can't; there isn't room. I can only dwell upon the tactics of Mr. Tutt long enough to state that at the conclusion of the case against Daniel Lowry, wherein it was clearly, definitely and convincingly established that Danny had been practising veterinary medicine for a long time without the faintest legal right, the lawyer rose and declared emphatically to the jury that his client was absolutely, totally and unquestionably innocent, as they would see by giving proper attention to the evidence he would produce—so that he would not take up any more of their valuable time in talk.

And having made this opening statement with all the earnestness and solemnity of which he was capable Mr. Tutt called to prove the defendant's good reputation, first, Father Plunkett, the priest to whom Danny made his monthly confession and who told the jury that he knew no better man in all his parish; second, Mulqueen, who described Danny's love of horses, his knowledge of them, his mysterious intuition concerning their hidden ailments, which, being as they could not speak, it was given to few to know, and how night after night he would sit up with a sick or dying animal to relieve its pain without thought of himself or of any earthly reward; then, man after man and woman after woman from the neighborhood of West Twenty-third Street who gave Danny the best of characters, including policemen, firemen, delicatessens, hotel keepers, and Salvatore, the proprietor of the night lunch frequented by Mr. Tutt.

And last of all little Katie Lowry. It was she who found the crack in Bently's moral armor. For Eleanor his wife was of Irish ancestry and of the colleen type, like Katie; and Bently had always played up to her Irish side when courting her as a humorous short cut to a quasi familiarity, for you may call a girl "acushla" and "Ellin darlint" when otherwise you are fully aware, but for the Irish of it, she would have to be referred to as Miss Dodworth. And this wisp of a girl with her big black-fringed gray eyes peering up and out over her gray knitted shawl, but for the holes in her white stockings and the fact that the alabaster of her neck was a shade off color—faith, an' it might have been Eleanor hersilf! It is obvious that any juryman who allows his mind to be influenced by the mere fact that one of the witnesses for the defense is a pretty woman—even if she recalls to him his wife or sweet-heart—is a poor weakling, a silly ass.

Otherwise all a crook need do would be to hire a half dozen of Ziegfeld's midnight beauties to testify for him by day; and the slender darlings could work in double shifts and be whisked in auto busses from roof garden to court room. Bently was no weakling, but Katie—perhaps because it was the moment of apple blossoms and dogwood and the anniversary of his wedding day—Katie got him. Kathleen Mavourneen, and all! No man could have brought up a fatherless and motherless girl like that and keep her so simple, frank and innocent unless there was something fine about him. You see, highbrows and lowbrows are all alike below the collar bone.

And here's the catch in it. Bently had told Eleanor that very morning that none of the rogues would get by him, and he had meant it. None of them ever had—in all his years of jury service. Time and again he had been the one stubborn man to hang out all night for a verdict of guilty against eleven outraged and indignant fellow talesmen who wanted to acquit. But quite unconsciously he found himself saying that this old fellow at the bar wasn't a rogue at all. If he was a criminal he was so at most only in a Pickwickian sense. All the previous cases in which he had sat had been for murder or arson, robbery or theft, burglary, blackmail or some other outrageous offense against common morals or decency. But here was a man who had never done anything but good in his life, and was at the bar of justice charged with crime merely because some cold-blooded mercenaries thought he was interfering with their business! Bently was in a recalcitrant and indignant frame of mind against the prosecution long before the defense began. The whole proceeding seemed to him an outrageous farce. That wasn't what they were there for at all! So swiftly does the acid of sympathy corrode and weaken the stoutest conscience, the most logical of minds!

Mr. Tutt did not put Danny on the stand—why should he?—and the octogenarian judge declared the case closed on both sides. Then everybody made a speech, in which he told the jury to disregard everything everybody else said.

Mr. Tutt spoke first. He thanked the gaping jury for their attention and courtesy and kindness and intelligence and for taking the trouble to listen to him. He told them what a wise and upright judge the old baboon on the bench was; and what a sterling, honest, kindly chap the fat assistant district attorney really was. They were the highest type of public officers—but paid—he accentuated the "paid" very slightly—to do their duty as they interpreted it. Now, Mr. Hingman would have to claim that Danny Lowry was a criminal; whereas, thank heaven! they all of them—every man of them—knew he was nothing of the kind! Criminal—that old man? Mr. Tutt raised his eyes and his arms to heaven in protest. Why, one look at him would create a reasonable doubt! But the case against him failed absolutely for the following reasons:

Daniel Lowry had not practised veterinary medicine without a license in taking care of Brown's sick horse, because he had not claimed to be a veterinary; he had not been paid for his services; and because all he had done was to help a suffering animal, as any man who called himself a Christian and had a heart would have done, and as it was his duty to do. Who "shall have an ass or an ox fallen into a pit"? and so on. It was in Holy Writ! The highest law!

There was no evidence against Danny at all, because Brown was an accomplice and his testimony was not corroborated; at any rate he was a procurer and instigator of crime, an *agent provocateur*, a despicable liar, hypocrite and violator of the very law he was paid to uphold; and as he had held himself out as a physician to Danny Lowry everything that passed between them was privileged as a confidential communication and must be disregarded as if it had never been said.

Daniel Lowry was a man of the highest reputation, of such character that he never had been guilty of an unkind or selfish act in his entire life, much less commit crime; which alone, taken by itself, was quite enough to interject and raise a reasonable doubt—upon which they must acquit.

Then Tom Hingman got up and grimaced and said he had known Mr. Tutt all his professional life and he was a peach, but they mustn't believe what he said or let him put anythin' over on 'em, for he was pretty slick even if he was a fine old feller. Now the plain fact was, as they all knew perfectly well, that this old boy had been caught with the goods. It might be tough luck, but the law was the law and they were all there to enforce it—much as they hated to do so—and there was nothing to it but to convict and let the judge deal with the defendant with that mercy and leniency and forbearance for which he was so justly famous. He panted a few times and sat down.

Then the judge took his crack. He told the jury, in so many words, to pay no attention to either the A.D.A. or to Mr. Tutt, and to listen only to him, because he was the whole thing. The question was: Had the defendant assumed to give medical treatment to Brown's horse, for any kind of valuable consideration? In determining this they should consider all the evidence, including the fact that the prisoner had claimed to be a veterinary, had been paid for treating Brown's horse as such, had pleaded guilty in the police court, and that none of the alleged facts upon which the charge was based had been denied before them in present trial.

As he said this the pink-and-white baboon looked at them steadily and significantly for several seconds over his eyeglasses. They should consider the business card which the defendant had given to the complaining witness and in which he held himself out as a veterinary. The testimony of the complainant stood uncontradicted. The complainant was not an accomplice and his testimony did not have to be corroborated. A decoy wasn't an accomplice. That was the law. Neither was what had passed between the complainant and defendant privileged as a confidential communication, because the complainant was not a physician. That was all there was to that!

They should ask themselves what in fact the defendant had done if not practise veterinary medicine without a license? It was not controverted but that he had said he was a veterinary, administered medicine to a sick horse, offered to compound payment for medical treatment for himself, finally taken five dollars, and admitted his guilt before the magistrate. If they had any reasonable doubt—and such a doubt might of course be raised by evidence of previous good character—they would of course give it to the defendant and acquit him, but such a doubt must be no mere whim, guess or conjecture that the defendant might not after all be guilty even if the evidence seemed so to demonstrate; it must be a substantial doubt based on the evidence and such a one as would influence them in the important matters of their own daily, domestic and business lives. That was all there was to it! Let them take the case and decide it! It should not take 'em very long. The question of how the defendant should be punished, if at all, did not concern them. He would take care of that. They might safely leave it to him! He bowed and turned to his papers. The jury gathered up their coats and straggled after Cap Phelan out of the court room.

"Y'd be all right, counselor," remarked the second court officer, suspending momentarily the delights of mastication, "if 'twasn't fer that son of a gun on the back row, Gibson! He's a bad one! I've known him for years! He'd convict his own mother of petit larceny!"

"So? So?" murmured Mr. Tutt, producing a leather case the size of a doctor's instrument bag from his inside pocket and removing a couple of stogies therefrom. "Well, it's too late now to do anything about it. I'm going out to stretch my legs and have a smoke."

Mr. Tutt loitered into the corridor, stepped unostentatiously behind a pillar, slipped into the adjoining court room—which happened to be empty—and thence back into the passage upon which the jury rooms opened. He found Cap Phelan standing before one of these with a finger to his lips.

"Pst! They're at it a-ready!" whispered Phelan as Mr. Tutt slipped him a stogy.

The transom above was open and through it drifted out a faint blue cloud. A great hubbub was going on inside. Suddenly above it a harsh voice rang out: "That ain't a reasonable doubt! I tell you, that ain't a reasonable doubt! Aw, you give me a pain, you do!"

"I've got 'em!" grinned Mr. Tutt contentedly. "Phelan, bring me a chair!"

Now right here is where this story begins—only here.

"Vell, gen'l'muns," said the foreman, who was a glove merchant and looked like Sam Bernard, as they took their seats round the battered oak table. "Vot you say? Shall we disguss or take a vote?"

"Let's take a smoke!" amended a real-estate broker. "No use goin' back right off and getting stuck onto another damn case! Where's that cuspidor?"

"Speakin' of veterinaries," chuckled a man with three rolls of fat on his neck, "did y'ever hear the story of the negro and the mule with the cough?"

None of them apparently ever had, so the stout brother told all about how—ha, ha!—the mule coughed first.

"I remember that story now," remarked one of the jury reminiscently while the fat man glared at him. "If I had my way all these veterinaries would be in jail!

By Advice of Counsel

They're a dangerous lot. I had a second cousin once who'd paid a hundred dollars—a hundred dollars!—for a horse and it got the colic. So he called in a veterinary and it died."

"Well, the vet didn't kill it, did he?" inquired the fat man scornfully.

"My cousin always claimed he did!" replied the other solemnly. "There was some mistake about what he gave the horse—wood alcohol or something—I forget what it was. Anyhow, I think they're all a dangerous lot. They all ought to be locked up. I move to convict!"

"But neither of these fellers is a veterinary!" retorted a sad-looking gentleman in black. "The charge is that one of 'em pretended to be—but wasn't. So if he wasn't how could you convict him of being a veterinary?"

"Well, if he had been I'd have convicted him all right," asserted the first. "They're dangerous—like all these clairvoyants and soothsayers."

"Will somebody tell me?" requested a tall man who had been looking intently out of the window, "whether a veterinary is the same thing as a veterinarian? I always supposed a veterinarian was a sort of religion, like a Unitarian. Veteran means old—I thought it was some old form of religion; or a feller who didn't believe in eatin' meat."

"Lead that nut out!" shouted somebody. "Let's get busy. The question is: Did this old guy pretend he was a horse doctor when he wasn't? I say he did."

"Let's take a vote," suggested Bently.

"Vell, let's understand vat we're doin'," admonished the foreman. "Do you gen'l'muns all understand that we're tryin' to convict this feller for doctoring a horse without a prescription?"

"You mean a license, don't you?" inquired Bently.

"Sure—a license. All right! Let's get a vote."

The first ballot resulted in seven for acquittal, four for conviction, and one blank—Bently's.

"I don't know who the fellers are that voted for acquittal!" suddenly announced a juror with a red face. "But I know this Brown personally, and he's all right. You can rely on him absolutely. He goes to the same place as me in the summer—Cottage Point. If any of you gentlemen want a good quiet place—"

"Any mosquitoes?" inquired an unknown irreverently.

"No more'n anywheres else near New York."

They took another ballot and found that the juryman who knew Brown had brought over two others to conviction, so that the jury was now evenly divided, Bently voting irresponsibly for acquittal.

"Look here!" proposed the man in black. "Let's argue this out. Suppose I put the various propositions and you vote on 'em each separately."

"Shoot ahead!" adjured somebody.

"Now, first, all who think this defendant claimed to be a veterinary say aye."

"Wait a minute!" interposed the tall man, who was still standing by the window. "Maybe I am a nut. But I wish someone would explain to me which is the defender. I thought Mr. Tutt was the defender."

"Oh, my Lord!" groaned a flabby salesman in a pink tie. "Defend-ant—a-n-t—remember your ant! He's the man we're trying! The other one is the complainant!"

"The only one that had any complaint was the horse", protested the tall man. "But I understand now—we're tryin' the defendant. I've never served on a jury before. Now, what's the question?"

"Did the defendant—ant—claim to be a licensed veterinary—when he wasn't?"

"Now wait a second," objected the tall man again. "I want to get this straight. Is it the point that if this old man pretended he was a horse doctor when he wasn't he has to go to jail?"

"Sure."

"But the other man pretended he was a doctor."

"But he was trying to trick the defendant."

"But the first feller wasn't a doctor any more than the other feller. Why not convict the first feller?"

There was a chorus of groans from about the table.

"You ought not to be here at all!" remarked the salesman acidly. "You're simple-minded, you are! You keep still now and vote with the majority, or we'll tell the judge on you!"

The tall man subsided.

"Vell," suddenly interjected the foreman, "he admitted he was guilty in the bolice gourt."

"Sure!" "That's so!" "Pass the box again!" came from all hands.

When the foreman had counted the ballots Bently was horrified to discover that ten jurors now thought the defendant guilty, and only two believed him innocent.

"May I suggest," said he earnestly, "that perhaps this old man did not understand in the magistrate's court the elements that went to make up the offense charged against him? He merely stood ready to admit freely whatever the facts were. His opinion on the purely legal question of his own guilt was not of much value. Anyhow, his subsequent plea of not guilty to the indictment neutralizes the significance of the original plea."

There was a murmur of surprise and admiration from Bently's companions.

"That's true, too!" declared the salesman. "I never thought of that! You're some talker—you are, I must say! But how about that business card?"

"It seems to me," argued Bently, "that the card plays no particular part in this case. In the first place the question before us is not whether Lowry ever did—in the past—hold himself out as a veterinary, but whether he did so on the day alleged in the indictment. The fact that he gave the detective a card which he had had printed perhaps years before only tends to show that at some time or other he may have pretended to be a licensed veterinary. And you will recall, gentlemen, that the testimony is merely that he said to the detective in reference to the card: 'That is my name.' He did not say anything to him about being a veterinary."

This somewhat disingenuous argument created a profound impression.

"Say, now you've said something!" declared the salesman. "You'd oughta been a lawyer yourself. Let's take another vote."

Curiously enough Bently's argument seemed to have had a revolutionary effect, for the jury now stood ten to two for acquittal. He began to feel encouraged. If ever there was a case— Then he heard an altercation going on fiercely between the salesman and Brown's summer friend, the latter insisting loudly that the detective was a perfect gentleman and entirely all right.

"Nobody questions Mr. Brown's entire honesty," interposed Bently hastily, in a friendly way. "The question before us is the sufficiency of the evidence. Upon this, it seems to me, there is what might fairly be called a reasonable doubt."

"And you have to give that to the defendant—it's the law!" shouted the salesman in fury.

It was at this point that Mr. Tutt and Phelan had taken up their positions outside the door, and the friend of Brown had told the salesman that he gave him a pain; that his doubt wasn't a reasonable doubt.

"Gentlemen! Gentlemen!" protested Bently. "Let us discuss this matter calmly."

"But I'm a reasonable man!" shouted the salesman. "And so, if I have any doubt, my doubt is bound to be reasonable."

"You—a reasonable man?" sneered Brown's friend. "You're nothin' but a damn fool!"

"I am, am I?" yelled the salesman, starting to remove his coat. "I'll show you—"

"Oh, cut it out!" expostulated the fat man complacently. "Settle all that afterward! We ain't interested."

"Vell, take annoder vote," mildly suggested the foreman.

This time it stood eleven to one for acquittal. All concentrated upon the friend of Brown, over whose face had settled a look of grim determination. But a similar expression occupied the features of Mr. Bently Gibson, erstwhile the exponent of the-law-as-it-is, the bulwark of the jury system, now adrift upon the ship of justice, blindly determined that no matter what—law or no law, principles or no principles—that old man was going to be acquitted.

"My friend," he remarked solemnly, taking the floor, "of course you want to do justice in this case. We have nothing against Mr. Brown at all. He is doubtless a very honest and efficient officer. But surely the good character of this defendant may well create a reasonable doubt—and the rest of us feel that it does."

"Sure! 'Course it does!" came from all sides. Mr. Brown's red-faced friend having escaped the salesman's wrath began to show somewhat less aggressiveness.

"I don't care a damn about Brown!" he assured them. "He can go to hell for all of me! But I don't see how you can acquit this feller when the evidence is uncontradicted that he told Brown he was a veterinary and treated his horse. I'd be violating my oath if I voted for acquittal after that testimony. I ain't going to commit perjury for nobody! I'd like to oblige you gentlemen, too, and vote your way, but I just can't with that evidence stickin' in my crop. If it wasn't for that—"

"He could 'a' treated the horse without doing it as a veterinary, just as Mr. Tutt said!" interjected the tall man.

"Good for you!" said the salesman, fully restored to equanimity. "You're gettin' intelligent. Serve on a few more juries—"

"But he said he was a veterinary," insisted Brown's friend. "How could he have treated the horse as anything else but as a veterinary when he said he was treating him as a veterinary?"

"Maybe he just thought he was doing it as a veterinary", commented the gloom in black. "He may have tried to do it as a veterinary and failed. In that case he didn't do it as a veterinary but just as a plain man. Get me?"

"No, I don't!" snorted the red-faced one. "That's all bull. He said he was a vet and he treated the horse as a vet and got five dollars for it."

"How do you know he did?" unexpectedly asked Bently.

"Because he said so himself. That was part of the conversation between Brown and Lowry," declared the obstinate summer friend of Brown. "If it wasn't for that—"

"If it wasn't for that you'd acquit?" demanded Bently sharply.

"Yes. Sure I would!"

"Then I say you should disregard all that conversation because it was a privileged communication between a doctor—Brown—and his patient—Lowry!" declared Bently heatedly.

"But the judge said it wasn't privileged!" retorted the other.

"Mr. Tutt said it was, though," shot back the salesman.

"Well, the judge said—"

"Let's go in and find out who said what," proposed the tall man. "I'd like to know myself. I don't remember who said anything any longer."

So they filed back into court.

"Your Honor," stuttered the foreman, licking his lips in embarrassment, "some of the gen'l'muns vant to inguire veder the gonversation between Mr. Brown and Mr. Lowry is privileged or veder we haf to belief it?"

The judge, who had evidently expected that the return of the jury was for the purpose of declaring the defendant guilty, scowled.

"The rule is," said he wearily, "that conversations between a doctor and his patient are privileged and cannot be testified to without the consent of the patient. If Brown had been a doctor—which he is not—it is possible that I might have sustained Mr. Tutt's objection on the ground and struck out the conversation. But he only pretended to be a doctor, and no privilege exists under those circumstances even if in some cases it seems to work a hardship upon the one who is deceived. The conversation in this instance is part of the record. You may retire."

But Bently, with a light upon his countenance such as theretofore had ne'er been seen on sea or land, suddenly held up his hand.

"One question, Your Honor. If Brown had been a doctor you would have excluded the testimony?"

The aged angel raised his eyebrows deprecatingly.

"Perhaps; I might have considered the suggestion."

"Thank you," said Bently, and they all traipsed out.

"That cooks him!" whispered Phelan to Mr. Tutt at the keyhole.

"Wait and see! Wait and see!" muttered the lawyer. "We're not dead yet."

Once back in their room the jury took another vote. Eleven to one again. Then Bently rose.

"Gentlemen," he cried, "I think I have the key to this case."

They all gazed at him expectantly.

"We are obliged by law to give every reasonable doubt to the defendant. Now the only obstacle to our acquitting this poor old man is the fact that there is in evidence a conversation in which Lowry is claimed to have said that he was a veterinary and had been acting as such all his life. Mr. Tutt says that that conversation is privileged and should be disregarded because it was a confidential communication between a doctor and a patient. The judge says it is not privileged for the reason that Mr. Brown was not in fact a doctor—but he says further that if Brown were a doctor we should have to disregard that part of the evidence—which would, as we all agree, leave us free to acquit.

"Now then, how do we know Brown is *not* a doctor? He says he isn't; but he lied about everything else he told Lowry, and he may have been lying about that too. And if he lied to Lowry he may have been lying to us here to-day. I say that there is a reasonable doubt right there as to whether Brown is really a doctor or not. Such a doubt belongs to the defendant. He is entitled to it and it is our duty to acquit him!"

"Hear! Hear!" "That's so!" "Bully for you!" "What yer got to say now, eh?" "Take a vote!" "Pass the box!" resounded through the transom amid a tremendous scuffling of feet and scraping of chairs.

"Phelan!" gasped Mr. Tutt. "Who shall ever again have the temerity to suggest that the jury system is not the greatest of our institutions?"

"Pst!" answered Cap. "Listen! Sh-h. By God! They've acquitted him!"

"So you caught the five-fifteen after all!" was Eleanor's greeting as the model juror jumped off the train. "I was terribly afraid you wouldn't! I hope you didn't let any rascal get away from you?"

"No!" He laughed as he leaped into the motor beside her. "Not a rascal! And I've got a surprise for you! I'm going to have my vacation after all!"

"Really!" she cried, delighted. "You clever boy! How did you manage it?"

"Well," he answered a little shamefacedly as he lit a cigarette, "the fact is that when the jury I was on returned their verdict this afternoon the judge said he wouldn't require our services any longer."

It was at about the same moment that two other good and true friends stood at the foot of the steps leading up to Mr. Tutt's ramshackle front door.

"Sorr!" Danny was saying in a trembling voice, the tears in his faded eyes. "Sorr! I would go to jail a hundred years and more, so I would, could I but hear again what they all said of me! Sure, I niver knew I was any account at all, at all! And them sayin' what a fine man I was, an' all! God bless ye, sorr! And whin ye stand, sorr, at the bar of heaven before God, the Judge, and the jury of all his holy angels, if there be none else to defend ye, sure old Danny Lowry'll be there to do that same."

Made in the USA
Middletown, DE
13 November 2017